Raising Little Leaders

Nurturing Leadership and Management Skills in Your Child

By: Mustafa Nejem

Foreword
Dear Aspiring Youth,

It is our greatest pleasure to introduce you to the life-changing adventures which lie within this book, "Raising Little Leaders: Nurturing Leadership and Management Skills in Your Child". Your choice to pick us as your guide is a choice you will never regret.

Since the world is developing at a fast pace, we understand the need to develop leadership and management skills in our fellow young friends. Our profound gratitude can't be fully expressed for entrusting us with delivering influential tales and moulding the minds of youngsters to be the next global leaders!

We aim to be the beacon of knowledge, treasuring engaging and captivating stories that are waiting for you. Open the book and ye shall find the adventures within that you can't turn away from.

Thank you for allowing us, the authors of "Raising Little Leaders: Nurturing Leadership and Management Skills in Your Child", to join you in the life-altering journey you will embark on.

Wishing you an exciting, adventurous, and uplifting reading experience!

With heartfelt thanks and enthusiasm,

Contents

Introduction

A warm welcome, my young comrades! You are about to step into the world of fellow students just like you, aspiring to be the leaders of the future. "Raising Little Leaders: Nurturing Leadership and Management Skills in Your Child" is designed to instill, enhance, and nourish the leadership and management qualities in the hearts of promising and ambitious youngsters.

Igniting the spark in each youngling is a crucial component to inspiring and motivating them. A spark that can only be ignited if they have something to relate with. "Raising Little Leaders: Nurturing Leadership and Management Skills in Your Child" comprises a bundle of enlightening tales, each designed to be captivating and, notably, relatable to the regular experiences of young, ambitious students. The book intends to ignite the fundamental spark in the hearts of its fellow readers, paving the route for leadership and management skills.

Each story has its distinct essence of adventure and learning, which your child can correlate with. Equipped with diverse morals, the book will share vital, knowledgeable lessons and aid in establishing a perception of the importance of leadership and management in life.

My young comrades, this book isn't an ordinary book at all. Part 2 of "Raising Little Leaders: Nurturing Leadership and Management Skills in Your Child" is loaded with immensely compelling and irresistible adventures. Don't just wait there; come on, hop in. Do you want to be the next coin champion, the courage captain, or any other influential leader? The "Tech Titan" title with your name would sound amazing! These activities will engage the youth in practical, collaborative adventures, further reinforcing the lessons taught in the stories and making leadership concepts more evident and helpful in everyday life.

We truly hope that this book becomes the medium that not only teaches but inspires, ignites the fundamental spark, enhances creativity, and develops all sorts of positive traits in the hearts and minds of our future leaders. The purpose lies in the name itself: raising your little child to be a leader by nurturing leadership and management skills.

May the stories of the Broad Classroom students enlighten you with insightful lessons, ignite the light within each of you, and inspire you to be the next passionate and confident leader!

Young Comrade, you are not alone! For I will always be by your side on this compelling adventure.
With Best Regards,

Part 1
Diverse Stories for Little Leaders

Chapter **1**

Leadership Basics

My enthusiastic comrades, we shall now throw the anchor into the water, stop our ship, and take our first step in the adventurous journey of becoming a strong leader. Are you ready?

Do you have what it takes to be a leader?

Before answering this question, we must understand who is actually a leader and what leadership means. A leader, in simple words, is a person who guides and inspires other companions to work collaboratively together to reach a shared objective. Imagine a leader as a kind friend who supports everyone, helps them stay on track by regularly checking in with them, and collaborates effectively.

Leaders demonstrate not only kindness but also justice and empathy to make sure everyone in their group feels respected and included in each activity. Whether it is about participating in different competitions, playing games with classmates, or completing homework together, a leader shapes the voyage into a joyful and memorable one while ensuring safety and concern for everyone.

Leadership is derived from the word "leader". Now that you've grasped who a leader is, you can automatically get an idea of what leadership is. A collection of skills and qualities required to be a strong and effective leader is called leadership. The simplest way to understand leadership is by considering it a superpower. A superpower that lies within each human being, which allows you to unite people as one, motivate them to work as a team, and guide the team toward the targeted objective. In essence, a leader is a welcoming guide, and leadership is the mystical ingredient that elevates what they say. It's all about collaboration, kindness, and helping one another achieve.

Now that you've gained some knowledge about leader and leadership quality, are you interested in becoming a leader? Remember, my friends, my first advice to you as your leader is always to be positive. Don't think that you can't become a leader, as everyone has the potential to be a leader and possesses leadership qualities deep inside their hearts. You just have to look for them, polish them, and make yourself a confident and compassionate leader.

Let's begin with the story of "Ivan, the silent student". Ivan's journey is one of the most inspiring stories you will ever know. He was a student just like you. Now, please pay attention, for the story is about to begin.

Ivan - The Silent Student

A simple child with social anxiety whose family moved into the neighbourhood where the Broad School was situated. His name was Ivan. Ivan, with his adorable and home-loving nature, sought comfort and a strong sense of security within the boundaries of his home. His love for familiar spaces was clear; he cherished the cosy feeling and the familiar rhythms that emerged within his home. However, an unforeseen problem occurred in Ivan's life which is frequent residence moves.

Despite his immense love for home, the regular changes in his residence made him quite uncomfortable. With every relocation, the soul of his soul haven diminished along with his cherished memories, the creaks of his favourite house, and the well-known nooks and crannies of his soul haven.

The ties he had established with his surrounding environment were broken consistently, and the feeling of peace he searched for became unattainable. Each new house brought its challenges of familiarizing with the new environment, removing the previous layers of comfort Ivan valued immensely.

"Happy 11th birthday, my son", Ivan's mom said while kissing his forehead and waking him up for his first day at school.

"Come on, Ivan. Get up, let's not be late on the first day, or else you will be remembered as the late boy. We don't want that, do we." his mom said, guiding him to stand up and get ready.

"Mom, it's my birthday. Can't I stay at home and celebrate my birthday?" Ivan said mournfully.

His mother shook her head and asked him to hurry up as he was running out of time. She thought he would be late, but as he was about to leave, they heard a knock on their front door. Without further ado, Ivan opened the door and saw a healthy boy who seemed to be of his age but a little shorter than him.

"Hi-i I…" Ivan stuttered.

"Hey, I am Dave, your neighbour. My mother is driving me to school, do you want to join us? She can drop you at your school, too.", Dave said with a pleasant smile on his face.

"Ahm…" Ivan was out of words; he wanted to carry on the conversation, but he was unable to do so.

Ivan's mother overheard the conversation and told Ivan to go with them, as she had previously met the neighbours. Ivan waved at her mother and left for the school with Dave. Little did they know that they were classmates from the same school, that is, Grade 7 Section A of the Broad School.

On the way to school, Dave continued to introduce himself further, which made Ivan comfortable knowing that they were of the same age and, luckily from the same school as well. Upon reaching the school, Dave expressed excitement, whereas Ivan was quite the opposite; he was more likely annoyed and bored. The bell rang, and all the students rushed to their respective classrooms.

"Well, Mom, I am on time.", Ivan thought to himself.

Dave introduced Ivan to his friends and was by Ivan's side throughout the day, guiding him about the Dos and Don'ts in the Broad School. For an introverted child disturbed by frequent relocations and social anxiety, having a friend like Dave would be a dream come true.

Dave was an extroverted student who was mostly bullied for being too talkative. All he ever wanted was to meet a friend just like him, a person who would care immensely about him, make unforgettable memories, participate in different activities together, and make life more enjoyable.

Meeting Dave on the first day developed a unique bond in Ivan's heart. A bond that was never to be broken, or was that what Ivan thought. Ivan's mother picked them up when school was over and bought them doughnuts as a treat for Ivan's birthday on their way back to their homes.

As days passed by, Ivan's mother started noticing a few changes in him. Unlike before, he developed a keen interest in his studies and became more willing to go to school. Was it because of the school or his friendship with Dave that encouraged him? Whatever the answer to the question was, his mother was grateful to see a positive change in his life.

"Ivan, are you good at any sports?" asked Dave as he stuffed his mouth with chicken nuggets.

"Did you say e-sports?" Ivan answered by asking another question. Dave was shocked by his enthusiasm, as it clearly indicated that either he was an amazing gamer or he just loved watching e-sports.

On sharing more about the upcoming tournaments which included both sports and e-sports too, Ivan was surprised that schools in his local vicinity encouraged video games. This was something he had never seen in any of the schools he had previously attended. Ivan expressed his love for competitive video games to Dave, but he was unsure if that was true, remembering how their first few interactions were.

Dave doubted Ivan based on his previous experiences with him, irrespective of how Ivan had changed as time passed by. Ivan used to be silent in class; he hardly engaged in any class discussions and activities. Expecting him to be a professional competitive video gamer, where the communication skills and leadership qualities of the captain must be on point, was difficult to accept.

The e-sports tournament was just a week away, the registrations were about to be closed, and the Grade 7 section A didn't even register. Each section was looking forward to winning in at least one category of the tournament, if not dominating the entire tournament.

Each e-sports team required a group of 5 students, 4 active players, and one substitute. Grade 7 section A was unable to register for the e-sports tournament because of a shortage of players in the team. They were two players short. Ivan wanted to participate but was procrastinating. He feared losing in front of a huge crowd. At this moment, his friend, Dave, came in handy and encouraged Ivan to sign up for the team. He further discussed with the organizers about letting their class register without a substitute player on an ultimatum that the team would be disqualified if someone from the team needed to be swapped. No one knew that this tournament would become a life-changing moment for the silent kid.

A week passed by, and the entire school was excited about the tournament. The event started with an orientation, and the prizes were displayed, creating hype and uplifting the participant's spirit to do their best in the tournament. Each category of the tournament, such as the spelling bee and other indoor and outdoor events, was organized in parallel. A student could be a part of multiple teams but they had to discuss it with the event organizers before their matches to avoid any clash.

The competitive multiplayer game in which Ivan and his team participated was the globally famous Fortnite. It is a battle royale game that initially has 100 players, and the last team standing wins. Each squad comprises 4 team members, and in a single match, 25 teams are competing with each other. The Fortnite tournament was about to begin in a few minutes.

Grade 7 A's team consisted of Ivan, William, Jeff, and Andrew. The majority of the class voted for William to be the captain of the e-sports team whereas Ivan received the least amount of votes. Despite it being discouraging, Ivan decided to stay focused on the game as it was the only thing he loved and excelled at. The battle began with a ferocious start, as 2 out of 25 teams were already disqualified within the initial 3 minutes.

Even though William was voted to be the captain of the team based on his communication skills, he wasn't communicating and leading the team as everyone expected. Rather than focusing on team play, he was obsessed with gathering the resources alone. Watching his gameplay enraged the other teammates, but Ivan maintained his cool.

Ivan decided to stay with Jeff and Andrew, just in case they needed any assistance. Soon enough, Ivan, Jeff, and Andrew came across a spot where a team was hiding and waiting for the opportunity to attack. "Oh No!" screamed Jeff with frustration as he got knocked down from behind.

Ivan's quick reaction time helped him locate the opponent team and react fast enough to shoot them down. Such an accurate and precise movement gained the audience's attraction. Everyone started cheering Ivan for his skills. Meanwhile, Andrew asked for support as he revived Jeff. Ivan's collaboration helped establish his team's trust more on him as compared to the captain.

Being appreciated by everyone across the room was a feeling Ivan was very unfamiliar with. He felt good and uneasy at the same time. Was it forcing the leadership skills that lay within him but were burrowed deep due to his previous experiences to burst out?

Moving forward, 11 minutes had passed since the match started and the safe zone area had reduced significantly. Grade 7 A's team managed to survive and be among the top 10 teams by hiding as the safe zone shrank. The remaining 9 teams comprised mostly of Grade 8, 9, and 10 sections. Being the only team from the entire Grade 7 made them a centre of attraction and put a lot of pressure on them. William stepped out of his cover under immense pressure and got knocked down. Upon being knocked down, he became mad at the team for not supporting and not being with him. This type of behaviour upset everyone except Ivan; he was well aware of what was about to happen.

Ivan was busy thinking about how to rescue his teammate, which seemed to be an impossible task. He politely asked everyone to calm down and started to take control of the situation. He began to lead the team by giving each member a specific role and a set of instructions to follow. Little did anyone know, this would alter the entire course of their gameplay.

Ivan, the silent student, was now talking to the team members in a confident tone. He became their leader who would explain each aspect of his strategy in a calm manner, which gained him more trust and respect. Following Ivan's commands, 7 A's team reached William in a matter of a few seconds. William was about to be eliminated, but thanks to Ivan's leadership, he was rescued by Andrew.

Everyone was amazed at Grade 7 A's performance and continued cheering for the team, specifically for Ivan. The safe zone circle was further smaller by this time, and all everyone could see was teams being eliminated. By now, 4 teams were remaining: Grade 7 A, Grade 9 A & B, and Grade 10 D. The final battle was about to begin for the winner of the Fortnite e-sports tournament.

Grade 10 D's team was the people's favourite as they were fighting head-on with each opponent they faced, whereas Grade 9 A was the least favourite as they were hiding through the entire game. Grade 7 A's team made the first move. They rushed towards an uphill and built a house with multiple traps inside. The entire team rushed to the first floor, whereas Ivan stayed behind to lay traps just behind the doors and near the staircase. Ivan joined the team when he successfully laid the traps and asked everyone to be alert.

"Ssshhhh", said Ivan slowly.

The team could hear someone approaching, and upon entering through the door, two of the opponent's team members got knocked down. Ivan told everyone to go downstairs and eliminate the entire team. He jumped out of the roof to come from the door, whereas his team came down from the staircase, sandwiching one of the 3 remaining teams and eliminating them. The team praised Ivan's call and high-fived him.

Just after a few minutes, they heard two teams battling against each other. Ivan came up with another plan to sneak attack the remaining team so they could secure victory. They slowly head towards the battleground while being unnoticed by the two opponent teams. Once the battle ended, the opponent team started collecting the super rare items. Ivan saw the opportunity and launched an attack on them. Despite having an advantage, Grade 7 A was about to lose the head-on battle but managed to be victorious at the very end. Grade 7 A had won the e-sports tournament! Everyone started shouting "Grade 7 A" and "Ivan" consecutively. Even though Ivan was a silent student with no friends except

Dave, he managed to win the hearts of the audience by emerging as a kind and compassionate leader in the tournament.

**** **** **** **** **** **** **** **** **** ****

My little leaders, as you can see leader, direct the team to attain a certain goal, and in the case of Ivan, he led his team to victory, even though he was a silent student. Remember, my little ones, anyone can be a leader, whether it is someone as silent and shy as Ivan or anyone else; you have to be honest, caring, respectful, and supportive of everyone. Don't ever think that you can't be a leader. Sometimes, it takes time to bring out your leadership qualities, and sometimes, it takes a while to polish them. There is a leader in every one of you! Now, let's sail towards our next adventure, Shaping Leaders of Tomorrow.

Chapter 2
Shaping Leaders of Tomorrow

My fellow companions, what do you want to be in the future? Is it a pilot, an astronaut, or your favourite teacher? Do you have something in mind? If yes, then tell me, is there someone who inspired you? Well, I want to be a teacher because I want to guide all of you to be the next leader of tomorrow! My parents have inspired me to be your teacher, as they used to teach me everything, what is good and what is bad.

Do you know what a role model is?
A role model is a person who motivates and inspires people by their way of life, behaviour, or achievements to set aspiring goals and live meaningful lives. For example, my role models are my parents. I want to be a teacher because watching my parents teach me everything when I was a child motivated and inspired me to teach and guide you on your way to becoming a leader.

A role model not only inspires but also portrays their beliefs and values. Youngsters look up to people who live as per their beliefs and values, making it easier to understand how personal values shape who they are and will be as adults. Such as students highlighted some famous personalities who helped advance technology to how it is today.

Rather than being self-centred, a role model is usually focused on giving more time to others, either by being active in communities or helping locals out. For instance, during the COVID-19 pandemic, local food businesses were affected the most, and some people reached out to help them in terms of difficulties.

Remember, my little leaders, positive role models have a very important role in your character development. Children learn how much effort is needed to achieve their goals, conquer the obstacles, and become a successful person. It helps in developing self-esteem which makes you more confident and do better with academics, socially, and emotionally.

The story of the two brothers, Max and Shawn, from the Broad School will illustrate the power of a sibling dynamic. Sometimes, there can be ups and downs between your siblings, but you should never let it ruin the strong bond you have. Instead of fighting against each other, fighting for the same cause is what made them the iconic "Clean and Green Brothers".

Max and Shawn - Clean and Green Brothers
Max, a student from Grade 9 B, was the elder brother of Shawn, a student from Grade 7 A. The brothers were very famous and well-known in school as the "Clean and Green Brothers". Not everyone knew the entire story of how they came to be famous and get such a title. Ivan was among those who didn't even know who Max was.

After winning the e-sports tournament, Ivan was the talk of the entire class even a week after the tournament. Ivan was still the silent guy he always was. He still used to follow Dave, be by his side, and talk to him only.

One day, he overheard his classmates talking about the Clean and Green Brothers, Ivan was very curious about what the story was behind their funny yet respectable title.

"It must be related to cleanliness", Ivan wondered to himself.

Ivan proceeded to ask Dave, and Dave replied that he would introduce Ivan to them so he could ask them straightforwardly. Hearing a positive response from his best friend brought a smile to his face. He was excited to meet the brothers and hear their story from them directly.

The next day, when Shawn arrived at the school, Dave reached out to him and asked for his time during the lunch break. Shawn, Ivan, and Dave agreed to meet during the decided time so they could hear Shawn and Max's story. Shawn started with the beginning of their journey.

Max and Shawn had a 3-year age difference; Max was 15, whereas Shawn was 12. They both used to fight each other as if they were sworn enemies. Whether it was a simple shared chore or a group discussion with the family, they wouldn't spend a single day without fighting. Max was a nature lover; meanwhile, Shawn had a keen habit of neatness and tidiness. It seemed like a case of peas in a pod, but the sibling bond wasn't as strong as it should've been.

Once, a group of university students organized a workshop related to environmental cleanliness and its benefits to all human beings. This workshop caught Max and Shawn's eyes; they instantly registered for the workshop presentation. The workshop also delivered knowledge about how students can influence others to discourage littering, promoting cleanliness and a better standard of life for all sorts of people.

While the workshop showed the facts to the students about littering and all sorts of pollution, Shawn was distressed. At the same time, Max was unhappy that the trees were chopped at a very fast rate, which no one could ever imagine. Both brothers were not pleased with how humans were treating the Earth. That's when they both saw a common objective despite their hard feelings for each other. This was the turning point when they decided to work together as brothers like they were meant to be.

The brothers embarked on a journey to make the Earth clean again! In the beginning, Max started organizing tree plantation drives, and Shawn helped his elder brother by gathering more young students to join. The tree plantation drive was the first successful program that Max and Shawn had organized. Following that, Max requested the school's principal to help him arrange a beach clean-up trip as the beaches are most polluted by whoever comes to enjoy the natural beauty of the sea. After weeks and multiple requests and letters from Max, the Broad School decided to organize a beach clean-up trip for all grades. Each section was accompanied by their teacher, and strict measures were taken for the safety of the students.

Before the school buses left for the beach, Max decided to deliver a motivational speech to all the participants and told them to do their best to clean up the environment. Upon hearing him, everyone stood up to give him a round of applause. The buses arrived at the destination, and the students were shocked to see how dirty the beach was. The fact that grown-ups litter everywhere was making the students unhappy.

Despite the unhappiness, everyone began cleaning up the beach. Specific tasks were given to each group, such as the first group collecting the trash, the second group accompanying them by holding the trash bags, and the third group aligning all the trash bags for the garbage collectors to collect easily. These processes, when done uniformly, made the beach clean-up trip very effective. Not only the students but the teachers were shocked to see the difference between the dirty beach and the beach cleaned up by students.

Upon return, the principal gave out certificates of appreciation to all the participants, which boosted the morale of all students. Inspired by Max's successful beach clean-up trip, Shawn decided to organize an awareness campaign for the whole community.

As it was Shawn's first campaign, he was unsure about its success. Shawn had low self-esteem and wasn't confident in himself. He was facing challenges from the community that made him upset. Max, based on his experiences, mentored Shawn and guided him to make his first awareness campaign successful. Under his brother's mentorship and cooperation, Shawn encouraged his peers to invite their friends and families in the community to attend the awareness campaign.

This resulted in a huge crowd showing up for the campaign. Shawn, along with Max, conducted awareness sessions regarding pollution, its causes, how to reduce pollution, and how reducing pollution benefits the environment. The community was pleased by the two brothers and decided to give them an award for organizing such a helpful awareness campaign. Their collaborative efforts led them to gain the title of "Clean and Green Brothers" by the head of the community.

The brothers were very proud of each other. Their journey of improving the environment, making it clean and healthy, not only gets them a title but also strengthens the bond between the brothers. Max's mentorship and guidance made him a positive leader for his younger brother, and their sibling dynamic gained them immense respect and recognition.

**** **** **** **** **** **** **** **** **** ****

My young friends, as you can see, even though Max and Shawn used to fight against each other despite being brothers, their transformation to fight for a common cause helped them grow immensely. Max became a positive leader for not only Shawn but everyone around him; in the meantime, Shawn's leadership qualities started to develop as he was given age-appropriate tasks. He became more responsible, cooperative, adaptable, and understanding. He became his brother's mentee and learned a lot from him, which helped him achieve the goal he set for himself.

Chapter **3**

Learning from Mistakes

No matter how good you are, there comes a point in life when you unintentionally make a mistake. My fellow buddies, making a mistake is natural; it doesn't mean the end of the world, but the wiser and more significant thing to do is learn from your mistakes. Learning from a mistake can transform it into a positive experience.

If I compare learning from mistakes with something, it would be your growth as a person. Mistakes can help you move forward, learn, and grow into a better person overall. You should learn from them and try to avoid the same mistakes from happening.

My courageous companions, I understand that when you make a mistake, the outcome is not what you were expecting. Not obtaining the result you were hoping for may make you sad and reduce your self-esteem.

But do you know what self-esteem actually is?

Self-esteem is a person's confidence in their own abilities. You should believe in yourself and your capabilities and be confident. When you have healthy and positive self-esteem, you can overcome all the hurdles in front of you because you can do it! It is easier to accept mistakes as nobody is perfect, and making mistakes and learning from them is a natural growth process.

Mistakes are just like challenges that you can overcome. But remember my young leaders, asking for help is also a leadership quality. Leaders are humans, too; they can make mistakes and ask for help. Collaborating with the team encourages them to contribute with more enthusiasm. In the end, leadership isn't just about guiding the team to achieve a goal, it has more purpose to it. Leadership promotes mentorship, as we read in the story of Max and Shawn, nurtures the growth of each team member, supports each other in terms of difficulty, and many more.

Following is the story of the Broad School's famous violinist, Sarah. A misstep in her musical performance led to her downfall. Let's hop directly into the story and know how she rose to the top.

Sarah - The Violinist

The Broad School was not only well known for its academics but also for extracurricular activities such as various types of competitions which include not only sports but also music. Each year, an annual music festival would be held in which students would either perform instrumentals or sing, and the winner would receive a trophy along with some cash prize.

A student from the Grade 7 A, Sarah found herself captivated by instrumental music. Whether it was a piano, guitar, or violin, it didn't matter, irrespective of what instrument was being played. Her love for music was unending. Sarah's love for music was a habit she inherited from her father who, himself, was a renowned pianist. He taught her about musical instruments, and upon looking at her interest in violin, he began to teach her how to use a violin. Years later, the family had a financial issue, which led to the end of her violin sessions with her father, as he would work multiple jobs.

The music teacher at Broad School was an all-rounder, excelling at multiple instruments. From violin, drum, guitar, and piano, she played each as if she had honed her skills from when she was a baby. The music teacher had to choose and finalize 8 participants for the annual music festival. She would conduct 3 trials before the main event to give every student a fair chance, and in case of missteps, she would consider giving the deserving students another chance.

Sarah was very excited about her first trials. She started training and practising weeks before it was scheduled. But there was an upsetting feeling within her heart; whenever she picked up her violin, it would remind her of the memories she had with her father. A deep breath was all she could take before her practice and the next moment she would be lost in her violin performance.

Passionate Sarah was now ready to take part in the trials. Dreaming of participating in the annual music festival and bringing the trophy to her home was the goal she wanted to achieve. No one knew what was about to happen in the trials.

"Sarah! Is Sarah ready for her trials?" asked the music teacher.

"Yes.", said Sarah politely.

Sarah walked up to the stage and stood in the centre. She saw the auditorium was completely filled; some students were just watching the performances while others were willing to take part in trials. Sarah looked at the music teacher, who was sitting in the front as a judge, and took a deep breath when she signalled her to start.

Keeping all the practice, goals, and her love for music in her mind, she started with a lovely and elegant start with a touch of nostalgic notes. The students, along with the music teacher, were shocked at how good her performance was, and a few even started gossiping about how she might be this year's winner. Just as a minute passed, Sarah unintentionally swung her hand with too much force, which produced a screeching sound. A sound that couldn't go unnoticed. Once the painful screeching sound entered her ears, she instantly stopped her performance and stepped down from the stage. The students wanted her to go on, but such a noticeable mistake left her embarrassed and disheartened.

Sarah's mind was filled with many negative feelings, such as disappointment and doubting herself. This moment became a turning point in her journey to become the winner of the annual music festival.

After the trials ended, the music teacher reached out to Sarah and wanted to discuss her performance. The soft-hearted girl couldn't take the burden of her mistake; she thought about what was left to discuss when she made such a mistake while playing the violin. Sarah shared the incident with her parents. Upon hearing about it, her mother told her to relax and explained that making mistakes is a part of life and is natural. What matters is your commitment to learn from your mistakes and to be better, taking the mistake and downfall as a source of motivation.

Her father walked out to their music room and started wiping dust off a curtain box. Sarah's mother asked Sarah to follow him. Sarah slowly and gradually tip-toed behind him so she could see what he was doing without being noticed. Sarah's father then pulled out a photograph from his teenage which showed that he was performing in front of a few people on a small stage in the corner of a room.

"No one used to listen to my music.", said her father.

He explained that initially, he used to perform in front of a countable number of people in a restaurant, but he never gave up. He started from scratch, learned everything by himself without any coach because his family wasn't financially strong, and managed to earn some cash for his performance. But as time passed by, he kept on practising and worked on his weaknesses. Eventually, the restaurant started to get full. People wanted to listen to his performance, and slowly and gradually, his audience increased drastically.

"It is okay if you made a mistake, my child. You have to work harder, learn from it, and try not to make the same mistake again.", said Sarah's father while he tapped on her back. Her father's words of encouragement brought a completely new spirit to life. She was more dedicated than ever to learn from her mistakes.

The next day, she met her music teacher. Her music teacher was very surprised and pleased to watch the liveliness in Sarah. She decided to give her another chance at the trials so she could see if she had learned from her mistakes or not. The next trials were to be held within 3 days. Sarah began to work on her musical journey, she started from the beginning by working on her basics and then moving onto advanced levels. In the meantime, Sarah tried to remember her performance and analyze where the misstep occurred. She placed her sheet music in her room and thoroughly examined the sheet. She went through the sheet and played the violin slowly and gradually, trying to identify her mistake.

Upon realizing what her mistake was, Sarah dedicated her practice time not only to the next performance but also to the previous misstep she made in front of the audience. She carefully began to work on her bowing techniques as it was the main reason that screeching noise was produced. Slow and steady practice allowed her to have more control of her violin.

Sarah's father helped her understand that music has an emotional connection to its artist. His advice allowed her to connect with her music and infuse her performance with more emotions. To improve her overall set of skills, she tried different practice methods and picked one that was the most effective.

As Sarah's self-esteem was reduced because of her bad experience, her father helped her boost it by recreating small concert environments. He would invite friends and families to attend his daughter's concert. In a park nearby, they would gather and watch Sarah play her violin. Even if there were any mistakes in her performance, each audience member would cheer her up and appreciate her performance. By doing so, she became confident and developed a stronger dedication to improving her violin skills.

Meanwhile, in the school, Sarah sought feedback from her music teacher. Her collaboration with her music teacher helped her identify her blind spots and refine her skills further. Practice-based on her teacher's feedback turned her better than she ever was.

During her progress, Sarah discovered the importance of self-esteem and learning from mistakes. She ensured that she had enough practice to not repeat the same mistakes. Her approach to practice on the quality of her work resulted in immense improvement. It also contributed to a positive self-esteem and a positive attitude towards her goals. Moreover, she began to treat herself with kindness. New Sarah, with strong self-compassion, could now tackle any challenges in front of her.

The day of the trials arrived; Sarah stood confidently on the stage and played the violin wholeheartedly. This time, Sarah didn't make any notable missteps and managed to impress everyone in the auditorium. Her performance secured her the 7th spot in the Broad School's annual music festival.

She couldn't hold her happiness inside. She kept thinking about the music festival from the moment when she was selected till she reached home. Her mother could see her smiling while walking towards the door. As her mother opened the door, Sarah hugged her instantly and gave her the good news. They called her father and informed him as well. When Father came home, he brought their favourite meals, and the small family celebrated the good news together. Upon finishing the dinner, her father whispered to her that you have to keep practising to win the annual music festival. Sarah nodded and hugged him tight, thanking him for everything he did for her.

Although the annual music festival was a month away, Sarah started her practice sessions again the next day. Finally, after a month of hard work, the day Sarah had always waited for that is the annual music festival had begun. She stood at the backstage, holding her violin tightly in her arms, and her heart was pounding loudly. At this moment, Sarah was feeling a burst of emotions such as excitement, nervousness, and joy.

She could recall her entire music journey from her childhood to her misstep and the day she was waiting for. As she stepped behind the curtains, the stage lights dimmed, and the spotlight was directed towards the centre of the stage. Sarah stepped into the spotlight, and everyone became silent.

A deep breath with eyes closed and the grip loosened, Sarah swung her bow. Her performance had started. An energetic start followed by a piece of sweet and elegant music that echoed in the auditorium and the hearts of her audience. The audience could feel the emotions in her performance, a skill that she developed with a lot of practice.

The students who attended her previous trials were shocked at how a student who made a mistake in front of everyone has now become an extraordinary violinist. The warm and touching melody filled the auditorium. It was hard to believe that it was the same Sarah from Grade 7 A. With a smooth ending, Sarah concluded her performance; she walked to the front and bowed, thanking everyone for listening to her performance. As she turned around and was about to leave the stage, a thunderous round of applause broke out.

This was an acknowledgement of her journey and how significantly she improved. Watching such a lovely response brought her to tears, and she stepped down from the stage with tears of joy. After all the performances ended, the results were announced by the judges and it was no surprise that Sarah was declared the winner of the Broad School's annual music festival.

**** **** **** **** **** **** **** **** **** ****

What a wonderful musical journey it was, wasn't it?

As you can see, my leaders, you have to first realize and identify your mistake. Once you know your mistake, accept it and learn from it. That's how you will be better and grow further into the person you've always wished to be.

Sarah, in her journey, lost her self-esteem because of a mistake she made, and it was not in her hands. Even though she was discouraged and disheartened, the first crucial step she took was identifying her mistake. With the help of her teacher and family, she managed to stand back up but stronger than before. She sought guidance when needed and it is essential when you are a leader. You must know when to ask for help and collaborate with everyone. A positive mindset and self-esteem are significant factors that contribute to your growth.

Chapter 4

Art of Young Voices

After reading Ivan the silent student's story, you must know how important communication is for leaders. Even if you look around yourself, there are many instances where effective communication is a must. Let's take your family as an example; when you are having family discussions, such as planning for a trip with your extended family, everyone's preferences and their available schedules are listed. Effective communication involves all the discussions that are done before the final destination and schedule have been decided.

So, my young leaders, effective communication is very significant not only in our daily lives but also in leadership development. It helps in shaping and polishing the leadership qualities such as inspiring, guiding, and influencing others. Communication is an essential component of leadership that helps achieve the desired tasks easily, promotes team collaboration, and contributes to personal growth.

Tell me, how would you tell about your goal to the team? How will you motivate your team members to give their best? How will you ask for help when you are in a bad position?

The answer to all such types of questions is through effective communication. Remember how William was talkative but wasn't effectively communicating with his team, and the team began to trust Ivan more than their captain because Ivan was leading the team with the help of effective communication.

Learning more about communication skills will help you understand the importance of effective communication. There are two types of communication skills: verbal and non-verbal. It means what it is. Verbal communication is one of the most powerful types of communication, that is, words or sounds that come out of our mouths. Speaking is the most effective type of verbal communication.

On the other hand, non-verbal communication is the message we deliver using gestures, body language, and other sorts of movements. The most effective type of non-verbal communication is through facial expressions, as a human can convey a vast amount of emotions without saying anything.

Have you ever wondered how your mom knows you are sad without you telling her about your sadness or concerns? It is because of your facial expressions. She can see your sadness through your facial expressions. Similarly, clapping is an example of non-verbal communication which expresses appreciation.

Back to another story about Grade 10 of the Broad School – it is now the final year for the students from all sections of Grade 10. Every student is excited to be graduated from school this year, but a teacher is a bit concerned about their students. Are they prepared for the future?

Grade 10 - The Final Year

Another ordinary day ended with the echo of the school bell which spread through the entire school. Upon hearing the school bell, students would hurry up and gather all their belongings so they could leave the school boundaries. The same routine occurred day by day until the last examinations were about to come.

As every teacher loves their students like their own children, similarly, a senior teacher, Mr. Sebastian, loved all his students and always wished the best for them. Mr. Sebastian used to teach Grades 8, 9, and 10, but as he grew older, he decided to teach the final-year students only.

The entire Grade 10 was soon to be graduated, so Mr. Sebastian wanted to equip them with the necessary skills that would help them in real life. Out of his love and concern for his students, he thought of different ideas to achieve his objective but failed to implement any.

Despite his failure, he kept on trying till he gave his students a parting gift, a gift that would help change their entire lives. Mr. Sebastian decided it was time for a change and listed down all the changes he would work on in the classroom while he was lying in bed.

The next day, Mr. Sebastian woke up with a spark in his eyes, which highlighted his enthusiasm and excitement to bring a change and give students the gift they deserve before they graduate. When he reached the school early in the morning, he carefully looked at the group of teenagers who were absorbed in their worlds and thought about meeting them after they were successful in life.

The new journey for the Grade 10 students was now about to begin as Mr Sebastian embarked on a mission to equip students with the necessary skills such as active listening, effective communication, and respecting diverse perspectives.

Instead of starting the day with a boring lecture, Mr. Sebastian kicked off with a discussion. He encouraged all the students to take part in the discussion by sharing their thoughts on a well-known, thought-provoking quote written on the whiteboard.

The students began exchanging opinions, and a lively and energetic discussion started. Some expressed their love for the philosopher, while others were busy challenging each other's perspectives. The diverse perspectives led to a fight among a group of students. Noticing such behaviour made Mr. Sebastian realize the need to prepare students for the future and assured him that he was on the right track.

To work on the lack of harmony and agreement in the classroom, he introduced conflict resolution sessions. Once a week, instead of academic sessions, he would conduct sessions related to solving conflicts among students. Students were taught the need to respect classmates while listening to their opinions and finding a mutual understanding between them. Regular sessions promoting harmony among students and discouraging fights helped create a safe space for healthy discussions and open dialogues. Whenever any conflicts arose among the students, they would implement what they learned and solve the conflicts with their new set of skills, empathy.

Apart from healthy discussions and open dialogues, team projects were introduced to help create a healthy and positive bond among the classmates known for fighting against each other. Alan and Rose were forced to work as a team because they were famous in their class for fighting multiple times throughout a single day. With the help of team projects and guidance from Mr. Sebastian, they were able to put their hard feelings aside. Eventually, as time passed by, Alan and Rose noticed significant changes within themselves. They managed to find common ground, work on the shared project, and finish it first. The teacher highlighted their example and explained the power of collaboration, active listening, and respecting others to the entire class.

Mr Sebastian became happy when he learned that his colleagues were shocked and praised the fast change among Grade 10 students. To polish their skills further, he replaced conflict resolution sessions with class debates. Each student was asked to pick a debate topic in a way that an alternative student could challenge. The purpose of introducing class debates was to encourage students to actively listen to opposing opinions and understand their perspectives while respecting them.

This experience not only enhanced the knowledge of the class students but also broadened their perspectives. A few students were convinced by their fellow opposing debaters and changed their perspectives.

Following debates, students were asked to form different groups and given various real-world problems. All group members had to effectively communicate, actively listen and respect the solutions to the problems. However, only one solution had to be submitted, which students managed to pick after a thorough discussion with the group members. There were problems whose solutions lay among those that were rejected by the team. This caused havoc, but as the student started to develop the skills of harmony and respect, they accepted their mistakes and promised to learn from them.

The gift Mr. Sebastian wanted to give to his students was already delivered to them, but before the students would realize it, he organized another event that involved the student's parents too. Different workshops taught parents about the importance of understanding their children's perspectives and engaging in collaborative activities. These skills are all connected to the leadership qualities students develop over time.

As the day of the last annual examination arrived, Mr. Sebastian woke up fresh, relieved of all his responsibilities, and sad to bid farewell to his students. Even though a student is acknowledged based on their academic performance and achievements, Mr. Sebastian focused the last month not only on preparing for exams but also personal growth of students and various skills such as effective communication, active listening, and many more.

On the last day, students gathered outside Mr. Sebastian's office and expressed their heartfelt thanks to him. At that moment, each student began to share their experiences during the last month of their school life. An unexpectedly strong bond was formed between the classmates, and the teachings of Mr. Sebastian left a strong impression in the hearts of the students. With the last note of the school year, the gift Mr. Sebastian wanted to give had been delivered, leaving an eternal memory of harmony, comprehension, and a changed educational experience that these youngsters would continue to benefit from for years to come.

**** **** **** **** **** **** **** **** **** ****

AH! I wish I was a part of that class. Don't you agree with me?

My passionate future leaders remember leadership isn't only about leading others to attain a goal. A good leader actively listens to all the team members respects their values, and effectively communicates with them. When you begin to understand and share the feelings of others, you will develop a connection with your loved ones, friends, and people around you. This type of connection helps create a supportive environment.

Empathy will help in enhancing your communication skills and enable you to express yourself more effectively. Positive and healthy connections with your friends and family will make you a compassionate and kind leader. Sometimes, it takes time to understand others, try to engage in healthy discussions, and don't get angry if their perspective is different from yours.

Remember, mutual understanding is fundamental in life. The teacher of Grade 10, Mr. Sebastian, focused on polishing the skills of his students by organizing different team projects, class debates, conflict-resolving sessions, and many more. This is because all of these qualities play a vital role in life, whether in personal relationships or professional life. A thriving community cannot be established without compassion, mutual understanding, active listening, and effective communication between the community members.

Chapter 5
Team Players in Young Hearts

As you know by now, being a leader is not limited to guiding others to achieve a certain goal but it also includes effective communication with others, actively listening, respecting others' perspectives, collaborating as a team, and many more.

My young companions, teamwork, and collaboration are directly connected to the path of a successful leader. Leaders who promote active collaboration among their teams gain numerous benefits not only for themselves but for the entire team.

Let me put you in a scenario and ask you a question. Let's say you are the most successful leader of your favourite company. You have a team that comprises members excellent in specific fields such as someone great at marketing, or someone great at inventing new products, and many more. Would you assign the one good at marketing to invent new products?

NO! No one would do that.

A good leader will recognize the strengths of their team members and create an environment for the team in which their strengths can be utilized well. In such a manner, the desired goal will be achieved at a better rate and with superior quality. This will also develop a sense of purpose and unity within the team, encouraging them to work together.

When team members come together to solve a shared problem, each member shares their unique way of overcoming the problem, making the collective approach of the team more effective. Collaborative environments encourage open discussions, active listening, and respecting different perspectives. A unique set of perspectives can help a team tackle complex problems and transform them into opportunities for learning and growth.

Now read the story very carefully as it will be an interesting adventure. It will further show how essential teamwork is and how it helps solve different problems as a team. Let's dive into the school world and see which adventure is next.

Grade 9 – School Camping

During the summer vacation, the Broad School organized a school camp for Grade 9 students. A camp that provides the perfect opportunity for Grade 9 students to experience interactions outside of school, learn their strengths and weaknesses, develop team-building and leadership skills, and use limited resources. The majority of the parents supported the school camp as it forced the students to step out of the digital world and be physically active by being a part of planned exercises and adventurous activities. Some students were excited about the school camp, whereas others expressed irritation.

All the students reached the school, and the school arranged buses to ride to the camp. The campsite was situated on private property, by a pond near the forest. On their way to the camp, students could see the early morning sun casting a warm shine on the tall pine trees, a sight they could never forget.

For a few students, this was one of the most eye-appealing landscapes they have ever seen in real life. Watching the scenic beauty ignited a flame within the students, and they became very excited about the adventures they were about to face. The students of Grade 9 had embarked on a journey that would test their current skills, give them a taste of practical life, and reveal the leadership qualities hidden within them.

Upon reaching the campsite, the drivers parked the buses and asked teachers to guide students to their respective camps under strict supervision. Each camp had a private camp guide, a class teacher, and the students who divided themselves into a group of 6. Before students could do anything, the camp guide asked for their attention and gave them a list of instructions to follow. Each student was asked to read it, and after 30 minutes, their respective guide would ask questions related to the instruction manual. Those who failed to answer the questions were asked to read the instruction manual and answer another question again. This ensured that the students were honest and read the instructions carefully.

The adventure guide informed all the students about the camp challenges, which involved crossing the pond, moving through the forests, and capturing the marked cliffs. Each student was asked to state their strengths and weaknesses, and even though students made their groups of 6, the guide remade and divided groups into groups of 3, but this time, it was based on the strengths and weaknesses of students.

In this manner, the newly formed groups of students were balanced, and the camp adventures would be fair and square.

There were a total of 12 groups from the entire Grade 9, each given an alphabet to identify them, starting from A to L. After the basic instructions were given, the students were asked to put their belongings in the lodge, and everyone had a healthy and nutritious breakfast on the large table just outside the lodge. Students were now prepared for the real adventurous journey that was about to begin.

The first part of the camp was crossing the pond; the group that crossed the pond fastest was to be declared the winner. This challenge demanded team collaboration and trust. The only way of crossing the pond was through a rickety rope bridge. By stepping on each wooden plank carefully and slowly progressing forward, each group managed to cross the pond, but one group, Group E, got everyone's attention.

James, Emily, and David were the members of Group E. On watching the previous groups walk slowly and carefully to cross the pond using the rickety rope bridge, David got an idea. He told Emily and James about his idea to run across the rickety rope bridge. Upon hearing such a dangerous idea, they both refused, but David was a naughty child; he had already made up his mind. As the guide blew the whistle, James started strolling yet faster than the previous groups. Emily followed James' tracks and managed to maintain a fast speed.

James was about to place his next step, and all of a sudden the bridge started to shake. James and Emily looked behind them and saw David make a run through the bridge. They began yelling, telling him to stop, but he ignored them. Just as he stepped on a plank at the centre of the bridge, it broke, and his leg went through. David was now stuck in the worst situation. Students who were watching him began panicking and called the teachers. As James and Emily were crossing the bridge at a faster speed, they reached the middle of the bridge and, with their team effort, managed to get David back up on the bridge.

Upon seeing this heroic act, now the students started cheering and celebrating when Group E crossed the bridge. The guide deducted points from Group E because of David's recklessness but gave additional points because of James and Emily's bravery and team efforts. But after what everyone witnessed, no one dared to run across the bridge. Luckily, group E was awarded the winners of the first part of the camp. All groups returned to the lodge after a thrilling adventure.

The next day started with another hefty yet nutritious breakfast early in the morning. Students woke up with a spirit of excitement as they knew the second part of the adventure was about to begin. Each group was given a map and a task to deliver a can of food to the marked location on their map. Walking through the dense forest and uneven terrain was a challenging adventure.

Group K comprised the most talkative students: Raj, Emma, and Sophie. The other groups underestimated Group K without knowing the strengths of the three. Raj always had a keen interest in hiking, Emma loved studying geography, and Sophie was the best problem solver from the entire Grade 9. Being talkative helped these three connect faster and better than others could.

Sophie took charge of the group and asked Emma to point out the best route for their team. Once Emma explained the entire route to the team, Raj gave them key tips that were very useful when walking through the uneven terrain. The effective communication and team collaboration between Group K gave them a head start that no one else had. The combined effort helped their group overcome any obstacle that came their way and be the first group to deliver the food can at the marked location.

As time passed by, all groups returned to the lodge but tonight was another special event. They lit up a bonfire and sat in a circle around it. One of the camp guides brought many packages of marshmallows and Graham crackers. Students rushed to get some branch sticks and stuck each marshmallow on the pointy end of the stick. The bonfire was used to caramelize the marshmallows and develop a brown, toasty flavour to it. The students placed the caramelized marshmallows in between Graham crackers and enjoyed their delicious snack. The students headed back to their lodge once the marshmallows were finished.

The last adventure of the camp was about to begin. Students were prepared to capture the marked cliffs but didn't realize the difficulty of this challenge until they saw it with their eyes. The camp guide demonstrated how one was supposed to climb the cliff and then tie a rope to something that could hold the weight of the other two team members and then guide them on the way up.

Climbing the cliff was a task that required excellent teamwork, as each member's involvement was crucial. Most of the groups decided to send their strongest link first so they could climb and tie the rope to something strong. The race to capture the cliff had begun. A member from each group raced towards the top of the cliff; some crawled to minimize the risk of falling, and the remaining took the help of their surroundings to progress forward.

When they reached on top of the cliff, students searched for heavy items around them so they could tie the rope around them. One of the students tied his rope around the trunk of a large tree. Upon watching him, the other students tried to tie their rope around the same tree, but the camp guide politely told them that only one rope could be tied around an object. The students then looked for other trees with wide trunks. Meanwhile, the others found huge rocks to tie their rope around.

The rope was pulled by the camp guide as a part of the inspection to ensure the other group members could use it to climb up the cliff. The loose end of the rope was then thrown down so the students could climb up the cliff with the help of the rope as their support. The remaining group members then slowly and gradually climbed their way to the top so their marked cliff could be captured.

The groups managed to capture the cliffs at the same time. Hence, the last adventure was a tie, and no one was declared the winner. The teams reunited at the lodge and were very exhausted. Most of the students instantly went to sleep, and the others talked to each other, strengthening their friendships. The school camp proved to be a catalyst for teamwork and leadership development.

The eagerly awaited last day of camp was finally here. The teachers and guides appreciated the combined efforts of the teams and their cooperation throughout the entire school camp. This adventurous journey inspired and encouraged the students to engage in more team collaboration activities. Teachers asked students to share their favourite moments of the camp. Each student highlighted a specific moment; meanwhile, the other students cherished those new memories. After the discussion came to an end, the camp photographer took a photo of the entire grade with teachers and camp guides—a photo which would be later distributed among the students as a memento.

The students were now armed with a better understanding of a leader and leadership qualities through teamwork and collaboration. The students were packed with a clear sense of accomplishment and thrill. This adventurous experience was the first step towards their physical and mental transformation. Initially, the faces were filled with displeasure and irritation, but by the end of the school camp, the same faces were lit up with true smiles and enthusiasm.

The challenges students faced during this journey forged better bonds among their classmates and created a strong sense of unity. They could reflect on the obstacles they overcame and the aesthetically pleasing landscapes they saw. Some students found new strengths within themselves, and some improved their current ones. As the sun started to set, the school bus left the camp for the school while marking an end to a thrilling and adventurous journey. This camp left them with a treasure full of unforgettable memories.

**** **** **** **** **** **** **** **** **** ****

Do you think they could've overcome those challenges without teamwork?

To be very honest, my aspiring comrades, some challenges can only be faced head-on with teamwork. With teamwork, you have someone to place your trust in and rely on. Take the example of Group K; all three members placed their trust in each other and, using their strengths, managed to complete the challenge first.

Similarly, James and Emily saved David from falling down the rickety rope bridge and still were the fastest group to cross the pond. Their teamwork stopped a major incident from happening, and David learned his lesson the hard way. Meanwhile, every group member trusted and relied on their strongest link to set up the rope on top of the cliff so they all could join them.

The school camp was not only an adventurous journey but a learning and growing one for the participants. The student's involvement in the extracurricular activities taught them how to apply teamwork skills to achieve the desired tasks.

Remember my young ones, team-based problem-solving activities improve critical thinking and help you realize the importance of effective communication, focusing on the strengths of your team members, and also implementing everyone's ideas. Overlooking a team member can lead to different issues and can even hold your team back from achieving your goal on time.

Chapter **6**

Dream, Plan, Achieve!

My future little leaders, you have heard a lot about setting a goal and working hard to achieve it. What is the goal everyone talks about so much? Is it something very important in life? How will a goal help in your growth? In this part of our book, we will develop an understanding of goals and their importance in your lives.

Let's begin with the stories we've previously read, Ivan who emerged as a leader of the team and had his goal set on the e-sports trophy. His hard work and dedication towards winning helped the team secure the victory. On the other hand, Sarah made a huge mistake in her trials for the annual music festival. She was heartbroken but with the help of her family's support and teacher's mentorship, she worked hard on learning from her mistake. She wanted to be the winner of the annual music festival and bring a trophy home so she could make her father proud. By setting her goal, she was determined to do her best to achieve it.

Does setting a goal give you superpowers?

Ha-ha, my youngsters, not really. But it does give you something, and that is "**a direction**".

When you set a target or a goal, in easier words, you get a clear direction of where you wish to go and what you wish to achieve. In this manner, your efforts will be focused on the direction you are aiming for.

Moreover, chasing a goal will give you an energy boost, which will drive you to tackle any problems in your way and commit you to your target. The process of going after a goal will make you step out of your comfort zone and encourage you to learn new skills and face real challenges.

As you overcome the challenges, you feel satisfaction, and once the goal is achieved, the sense of accomplishment is no less. Accomplishing smaller goals can lead to goals with a greater purpose in life. The next day, you will wake up with enthusiasm shining on your face and next-level energy.

Goals should be aligned with your interests and passions for many reasons. The top 3 reasons are that your commitment to achieving this type of goal will increase by a huge margin, your creativity will increase, and it has a better impact on your positive mental health and gives a boost of self-esteem once fulfilled.

One of the best ways to set goals is with the help of interactive activities within the family. Family fitness challenge promotes a healthy lifestyle and teamwork. Tracking everyone's progress and celebrating small achievements together strengthens the family bond and enhances personal growth.

But what if you have to take matters into your own hands, my young leaders?

Wade, the unhealthy kid, came across a medical emergency. An emergency that could only be taken care of if he wills. He had his parents' support, but his commitment and hard work were the only ways he could overcome this issue. Let's read more about Wade and his journey to be the better version of himself.

Wade – The Unhealthy Kid

Wade was a student in Grade 7A, just like Ivan was named the silent kid; he was named the unhealthy kid for obvious reasons, which was his unhealthy diet. Wade loved food, but his love for food changed him drastically. He gained excessive weight and was categorized as obese by the doctors. Obesity had a negative impact on his daily life; a student who was physically active and mentally positive was now a lazy and overthinking student.

On a certain day, he fainted during a class, an ambulance was called, and he was rushed to the hospital. The doctors emphasized a change in his lifestyle and told his parents to strictly monitor him. Upon waking up, he saw his mother crying in the corner of the room, and as she noticed he was awake, she quickly wiped her tears and asked how he was doing.

The view of her mother crying made him not only emotional but motivated him to set a goal. A goal that would change his lifestyle and make him an entirely different yet new version of himself. When he got discharged from the hospital, his parents took him home and calmly explained to him about his health condition. Hearing about his health in detail made him concerned for himself, and he set a target to bring a major change in his life.

The realization of the need for change was the first step in the journey he was about to embark on. Wade began searching for health, fitness, and wellness campaigns in his nearby areas. He came across a few, but they were very expensive, and he didn't want to be a burden on his parents. Just as he was about to give up his search for a cheap health fitness and wellness campaign, his father sent him a poster about a health fitness campaign going on around the next block.

Wade couldn't hold his happiness inside; he went straight to his father and thanked him for his help. The same day, Wade got in touch with the campaign organizers and shared about his health with the fitness coach. The fitness coach was touched by Wade's goal and decided to help him in his journey without any fees.

The campaign had proper plans tailored for the participants based on their weights. Some included extra physical activities and nutritious meals, and some with activities to blend in with daily life. As Wade loved unhealthy food and would crave food throughout the entire day, the coach made a custom plan for him. Wade's fitness plan included a longer duration of walking, fewer sets of exercises, and delicious yet healthy food.

Wade was very excited to bring a change in his life for himself and his parents. He started the next day by making his own healthy and nutritious breakfast. He also prepared lunch that he could enjoy during his school break.

Wade was happy, but as he had his lunch, his smile began to fade away. He could see everyone around him having unhealthy yet tasty food. He found it harder to resist despite having a nutritious lunch. His classmates were shocked when they saw him have a healthy meal and started to make fun of him without any reason. Ivan noticed the look on Wade's face and stepped in to stop the students from making fun of Wade. Ivan went to Wade and put his hand on his shoulder and told him that he was doing great.

These words of assurance ignited the fire within Wade's heart and revived his commitment to achieve his newly set goal. After returning from school, Wade headed to the fitness camp and met his coach. He shared about the first day of his plan and started working out as instructed in his plan. The coach appreciated his efforts and motivated him to keep up the good work.

Wade was beginning to step out of his comfortable daily routine and step into a hardworking yet helpful one not only confined within the gym but his home too. His parents, fitness coach, and the gym's environment were now his source of motivation to be physically and mentally healthy.

His physical strength began to increase as he got used to his tailored exercise routines and overcame the challenges given to him during his workouts. The daily exercises involved focused breathing and rest between the sets, allowing him to maintain his composure. A balanced, nutritious diet supported him in achieving his fitness goals.

As weeks passed by, Wade was able to notice the change within himself and was further motivated to see his weight reduce. He could feel the desire to work harder to reach his ultimate goal. Even the slightest physical transformation felt as if he had accomplished something great. To others, it wasn't much, but to him, it was something incomparable because he went through every step of his transformation.

The change in Wade's body became more visible and shocking for not only his classmates but also other Grade students from the Broad School. He started to get appreciation from random strangers. Those who made fun of him were now showing him off as their friends. It made Wade giggle and motivated him enough to make his enemies shut up by becoming a better version of himself.

Wade was more determined than ever. His determination helped him get closer to his goal. His coach made his custom fitness plan a bit harder by adding a bunch of exercises for a longer duration of time. Cardio training, training with resistance bands, and high-intensity workouts were added to his previous plan, shaping his old plan into a more challenging one.

Being around people with different backgrounds in the gym, each with an inspiring story, made it easier for Wade to blend in, unlike his school in which students made fun of him instead of supporting him. There were different group fitness challenges in the gym, which added fun to this hard journey. The shared energy and together movement towards the fitness goals developed a sense of unity within their hearts.

Months had passed by now; Wade was at the top of his fitness journey with his confidence held high. He was now standing in the centre of the gym, surrounded by the same people who motivated him in his journey. Soon, he was able to remember his past and how much he had achieved. This Wade was far away from the old one – someone strong, fit, positive, and healthy guy yet with a soft heart for everyone around him as he could share what others had felt.

On his last day of the health fitness and wellness camp, Wade met his coach after months of dedicated training. He decided to remind his coach about his fitness journey, his struggles, and his commitment to his goal. Wade was full of emotions; he was excited yet sad as it was his last day at the gym. To his surprise, his fitness coach, with a wide smile on his face, revealed to Wade that he had been through the same path Wade was on. But unfortunately, he didn't have any coach to guide him and that was the main reason why the coach allowed him to participate in the camp without any fees.

With eyes full of tears, Wade hugged him tightly and was grateful for his support on this hard journey. The coach appreciated his dedication and his transformation. This secret established a strong connection between the coach and his trainee. But for Wade, his fitness coach became his inspiration and motivation to do better.

He realized that he had aligned his goals with a newly developed passion for health and fitness. Now, the custom plan was just a part of his daily routine. His journey was so inspiring that he was given an award in school. His peers couldn't believe that it was the same unhealthy kid at the beginning of Grade 7 A. Wade outgrew his old self into a responsible and healthy kid. His mother was so proud of her son that she began sharing about Wade's transformative journey with his relatives, friends, and neighbours.

**** **** **** **** **** **** **** **** **** ****

What an inspiring journey!

As you can see, Wade was just an ordinary student who was unfortunately obese because of his unhealthy eating habits. In the case of an emergency, he realized the need for a change. He set his goal and focused on achieving it. In the beginning, the journey was quite rough; all he needed was a little push, and his transformative journey got a boost. This boost wasn't a superpower, let me assure you. He was just determined to achieve his goals and had a direction to follow. Setting a goal had a major contribution to his personal growth and the transformative journey.

My young and energetic comrades, in order to be something, you must set a goal, and that goal will make a clear path for you to walk on. There might be hurdles on this path but you have to be strong, committed, and do hard work to get to the target. Once you hit the target, you will feel as if you accomplished something and will never forget that moment.

Have you participated in any races? If yes, that's great. You know everyone in the race wants to come first. Even if you secure a position within the top 3, you feel excitement and a sense of accomplishment. Similarly, goals aligned with passion or interest increase the feeling of accomplishment immensely.

Remember, to effectively set a goal, you must follow the SMART rule. SMART goals stand for goals that are specific, measurable, achievable, relevant, and time-bound. You should know precisely what you wish to achieve, and that is a specific goal. Breaking down a goal into smaller and more attainable goals that can be tracked and celebrated is the purpose of having measurable goals. In this manner, you can track your progress.

A goal must be realistic, no matter how challenging it is. An unrealistic goal has a few chance of being achieved, and if a goal isn't achieved, it reduces your confidence. So, my enthusiastic and energetic kids try to set an achievable goal. Goals that align with your interests are relevant, and setting a time limit for a goal makes it time-bound.

Now that you have learned the SMART rule of setting goals. Make sure you achieve them all; I wish you the very best. Don't give up, and stay focused. You can overcome any problems that you encounter; some may take time, and some will be instantly solved.

Chapter 7

Tick-Tock Win

Wade's fitness journey made me shocked, too just like his classmates. We all know it must have been hard for him, but setting a goal made it easier for him. Just as setting a goal effectively is important, time management is also important.

Time management is a crucial component if you are to be a future leader. Leaders have to guide teams to achieve goals but there is a time-bound too at majority of the occasions. Using your time wisely and effectively can help you move on track to your desired goal at a faster pace, saving time for other goals or relaxation.

By managing your time well, you can set priorities on tasks and do them within the deadline based on what is more important. My young comrades, you are just being smart with the time if you are managing it well.

Let's say you are stuck on a certain topic in mathematics; what will you do? You will break it into simpler parts that you can easily manage; in this manner, you will manage your time accordingly. The result will be you acing the next mathematics test on the same topic.

Students can get ample time to study, do their homework, and prepare for exams. In the meantime, doing household chores will instil responsibility and encourage a tidy and well-organized living environment. Taking breaks between these activities will help improve mental well-being.

Good time management skills have many benefits, such as increasing productivity and efficiency, balancing work and entertainment, reducing stress, and improving decision-making ability. These benefits will help you lead a stress-free and healthy life.

Let's hop into the well-advertised marathon in which a few students from the Broad school were willing to participate. Did they finish the marathon? If yes, how did they manage their time and efforts? So many questions come into mind, as the students are just so young, and a marathon can drain even an active and energetic adult.

The Power Squad – School's First Marathon Relay Team

Watching their classmates make so much progress, a group of five close friends from Grade 7 A, Lucy, Ken, Paul, Rick, and Ava, were encouraged to make a name for themselves. They collectively decided to name their group "The Power Squad". Each member of the power squad was extremely skilled, but not in academics. The Power Squad wanted to be recognized not only by their school but also by the entire town. So, they began to search for any events or competitions happening nearby. Eventually, they came across a marathon relay organized by the neighbouring town.

The Power Squad members are comprised of friends with diverse backgrounds and unique personal goals, excluding the collective goal of being recognized. Lucy belonged to a poor family; her parents struggled a lot to earn some money. She would help them after school. In this manner, the burden on her parents was reduced to some extent. Even though Lucy was young, her commitment to helping her parents was strong. The only issue she was facing was maintaining a balance between her school, work, and leisure time. Lucy took almost no leisure time which caused her stress and weakened her physical wellbeing state.

Ken was a guy who would always keep his cool even when in the worst conditions possible. He would plan everything, but it never produced the expected results. Even in failure, he would maintain his composure. Unfortunately, this attitude was good for his mental health but didn't help in achieving any target, and he lacked the dedication to work.

Paul was an energetic kid, always seeking a thrilling adventure. His excitement for adventures compromised his study and work capabilities, as he would leave his chores and homework unfinished. His habit angered many people close to him, but he didn't care, no matter how much he was scolded.

Rick was a determined student, who would focus on his studies only even in his spare time. As he wasn't good at academics, he spent most of his time trying to improve his academics. Unluckily, the pace of his academic growth was awfully slow, and watching this was very frustrating.

Unlike every other member of the Power Squad struggling with physical or mental well-being, Ava struggled with time management only. As she was a runner who competed in the school's racing events, she had to practice regularly. Ava wasn't able to manage time for her studies and practice sessions, which resulted in bad grades.

Lucy needed some leisure time along with the balance between studies and work. Ken required a push that would help him reach his goals. Paul had to begin focusing on work and studies more rather than leisure time. Rick wished for some time out of academics, and Ava wanted to manage her time well for her studies.

Each member of the Power Squad was determined to achieve their newly established goal. They began preparations for the upcoming marathon relay driven by their personal goals. As no one except Ava knew about the marathon relay, they had to be briefed. Ava took the first significant step in the preparation by explaining the rules and regulations of the marathon relay to everyone.

"Isn't it just a simple race?" asked Rick.

Everyone nodded as they heard Rick and needed some clarification. To which Ava responded, "Yes, in simpler words it is just a race, but no ordinary one."

Her response shocked everyone yet made them excited at the same time. Ava further explained how a marathon works and how a runner has to maintain his/her pace instead of just racing forward till the end. She motivated everyone to do their best as they needed to make a name for themselves, and the journey that the Power Squad was about to embark on wouldn't be as easy as they thought.

Everyone started working on the second step, which was the hard training for the upcoming marathon relay. Ava suggested everyone take at least an hour out of their busy schedules and use that hour efficiently to train themselves. Lucy, with a heavy heart, shared her collaborative team goal with her parents and asked them if she could take an hour out of her work. Her mother got emotional because she felt that the adventures Lucy should be enjoying during her young age were stopped because of their financial problems. Now that Lucy asked for an hour out, her parents agreed, supported her goal, and wished her luck for the training and the marathon event.

Ken was calm about the marathon, but his recent failures had ignited a desire in him to achieve this new target. He was more dedicated than ever to participate and secure a good position in the marathon relay. Ava's words and motivation gave him the push he had always needed to perform better and achieve the goals he had set. He started by setting specific time schedules for his training while balancing his studies and leisure time.

Similarly, Paul's energetic spirit had him excited for the marathon relay event. Unfortunately, his annoying behaviour made it difficult for his mother to allow him to the event. She put an ultimatum that she would only allow him if he established a habit of completing all the chores and homework within the assigned time. Her condition made him weep, but he had to agree to it for the target the Power Squad had set.

Rick was so stressed about his academics that he was on the verge of giving up because of his awfully slow growth in academics. As he needed some time for his physical and mental well-being, he instantly agreed to take an hour for the practice sessions. Ava decided to invest another hour in teaching the Power Squad about the marathon relay and give them some tips to win.

The marathon relay was a month away. For some, this might not be enough time to begin from scratch and take part in the event, whereas for others, this might be just a perfect opportunity to test their skills. Random questions would pop into their mind during their training sessions, but as their main focus was training, they would put those questions aside for some time. Ava would later answer each question at the end of their training sessions. Every group member, including Ava, was currently facing problems with conflicting priorities, as taking out time for something new wasn't their habit.

As time passed by, each individual began to develop a habit of practising for an hour. No matter what the emergency was, they would manage time efficiently and prioritize tasks according to their importance. By the end of the month, Power Squad was prepared to achieve its goals by winning the marathon relay event in the neighbouring town.

The eagerly awaited marathon relay day had arrived. As the marathon relay is beginner-friendly, Ava wasn't as concerned as she was initially when the Power Squad had no knowledge about it and had no marathon training. Ava woke up early in the morning and reached out to the team; upon hearing from everyone, she asked her parents to pick everyone up from their homes and drop them off at the marathon relay event.

The Power Squad was ready for the event they had been direly waiting for! Everyone lined up at their respective starting points, and the order of the Power Squad in the marathon relay was Ava, Ken, Lucy,

Rick, and then Paul. The marathon was about to start in a few moments. A decent amount of participants showed up but most of them were adults. Once everyone was lined up properly, the event organizers started a countdown from 10. Just as they reached 0, a starter's pistol was fired, and the marathon relay started.

All the marathon runners started with a good pace, some leading others and the others falling behind. Ava decided to start at a slower pace as compared to others. She wanted to contain her energy within herself for some time and find the perfect opportunity to let it all out. As she reached almost half of her leg, she noticed that the majority of the runners had slowed down. A perfect opportunity is what she thought to herself and raced forward with her entire strength to finish the first leg as fast as possible. She could see Ken jumping and waving while shouting at her not to give up! Hearing his words boosted her spirit, and she raced faster towards him. Ken was ready to take the relay from Ava and start his leg of the marathon.

This time, Ken wanted to give his best for the Power Squad's goal as he was done with his previous failures. Just as he got the relay from Ava, he appreciated her effort and began to run at a fast pace from the beginning. Despite the intense training, he had forgotten one of the most basic tips that is marathon is not just about reaching the finish line. Sadly, just as he reached the half of his leg, he was out of breath and stamina. He was struggling to push through. He could see Lucy far away, but out of breath, Ken just stood at the corner, trying to catch his breath. This pause was very costly as the other marathon runners were catching up. Ken got a glimpse of his previous failures in his mind, and he used that moment to motivate himself to run till the end. He slowly started to catch up with the runners who just crossed him, and soon he handed the relay to Lucy.

Lucy softly told Ken not to worry about the marathon and to rest so he could catch some breath and feel better. After watching Ken's leg, Lucy realized the importance of managing a proper pace during the marathon. She maintained a balanced speed throughout her leg but wasn't able to overcome a good amount of runners. She gave Rick the relay, and Rick followed in her footsteps. But at the end of his leg, he tried to run a bit faster so he could be among the top 8 marathon runners. Luckily, as he made it among the top 8, his leg was about to end, and he gave his relay to the remaining member of the Power Squad, Paul.

Ava made this lineup based on the physical activeness of the team members. She knew the beginning and the last leg should have strong runners, so she placed herself at the beginning, which gave the team a head start, and Paul at the end so he could fulfil his thrill and help the Power Squad achieve their goal. As Paul received the relay, he made up a scenario in his mind about how he could win the race. With random calculations and thoughts in his mind and a direction toward the team goal, he managed his time according to the goal requirements. The other runners were losing their pace as they raced towards the end line of the marathon. With a huge leap of faith and a deep breath, Paul tilted his body forward and began to run fast. As an enthusiastic guy who loved thrilling adventures and had a good amount of experience, he knew how to manage his breath while running. Paul raced through the other runners and was able to come first just at the right nick of time.

Paul could hear the cheers of the crowd grow louder as he was about to be the winner of the marathon. The crowd was encouraging him to move faster and take away the victory. He sprinted towards the finish line, breaking through the ribbon and making the crowd erupt into a great round of applause. A feat that has never been achieved, a bunch of Grade 7 students won the town's marathon relay!

Paul lay down in the middle of the road, gasping for breath. Lucy, Ken, Rick, and Ava rushed toward the end line, and upon seeing Paul lying down, they lay beside him. Just after a moment, Ken said, "Finally, a successful moment", and laughter erupted among the Power Squad. As it was a town's marathon relay event, it was well-advertised. Media was present to broadcast the marathon to the community members, and as the winners were finalized, they took interviews of the groups.

Through media, the feat became viral and the Power Squad became more famous than they even aimed for. The school awarded them with a trophy, and they received cash prizes from the community.
**** **** **** **** **** **** **** **** **** ****

I ran out of breath when I read about Ken. I thought the Power Squad would lose…

My young children, you know, running a marathon itself delivers the importance of time management. You have to maintain a pace in such a way that you don't get burnt out or exhausted, just like managing time. Sprinting doesn't lead to success every time sometimes you just have to maintain a steady pace.

During the marathon, the runners had to make good decisions while allocating time effectively along with resources.

Each story character was going through difficult phases of life, but they had to manage time in a way that they could get an hour for their practice sessions. Lucy balanced her study, work, and leisure time routine by reducing an hour from her excessive work so she could work on something else that would help her physically and mentally.

Remember, my comrades, sometimes managing time isn't possible without any support. Some individuals struggle with managing time effectively in the beginning, but with their friend's collaboration and support, they begin to allocate time and manage it well.

Nowadays, as technology is growing on a regular basis, you can download multiple applications or software that could help you organize yourself and manage time properly. By tracking down how you spend your time daily, you can analyze how well you are doing. If you feel that you are not managing your time well, you can break down your tasks and do them within a certain time limit. Using the technology around you properly can aid you in your daily life as well.

I hope you will begin utilizing your time well. Don't let me down; I believe in all of you!

Chapter 8

Superpowers of Decision-Making

Isn't it a lovely journey towards becoming a future little leader? By now, you must have learned a lot of lessons from the stories within each chapter. In this chapter, we will be learning about decision-making and its importance.

If we break the term decision-making into two parts for better understanding, we will obtain "decision" and "making". A decision can be defined as a choice that you make, and making is a verb. In simpler words, the process of making a choice is decision-making. My young companions, our decisions can affect different people in one way or another. That's why there is a need to make informed decisions; in such a manner, people will have an understanding of the possible outcomes of the decision.

Let me share a few steps to make effective decisions in your life.

You should begin by identifying why the decision is important and list down its possible outcomes. This will help you understand what is beneficial for you and what is at stake. This process is named as clarifying the situation. You can clarify the decision-making process by asking yourself a couple of questions.

After you know about your choices and their outcomes, evaluate each option you have. Look inside each option and gather information about whether it will be right for you or not and why. Once you have made yourself familiar with the choices and their outcomes further, it will make the final decision-making process a lot easier.

After making your final decision, don't forget to learn from the results. Sometimes, the results can be in your favour and sometimes not, so don't be discouraged; instead, make a better decision next time.

Good decision-making skills in life can help you get better results and new opportunities to grow. It also means that you are committed to learning from your mistakes rather than making the same mistake again and again. My young children, these skills are important to be an effective leader as well!

Another chapter, another story. This story will teach you numerous things and equip you with skills that will also benefit you in the future as a leader. The teachers of Broad School have now organized an event that will help these young students learn new and effective leadership qualities.

Broad School Needs a Savior

As the next session started, Broad School came across a unique issue that had never been encountered before which is a financial issue. The school has been well-known for academics and extra-curricular activities. Everything was going smoothly until one day, the investors reduced their school's budget, which paused a few ongoing events. The pause made students, parents, and even the faculty members upset as these events were necessary for the physical or mental well-being of the students. The administration of Broad School tried their best to resume the ongoing events and make the necessary changes in the budget without compromising the reputation of the school. Unfortunately, the budget crisis news spread through the entire school, making everyone concerned.

Every teacher could hear their students gossip about the budget crisis in the classrooms and even during school breaks. In a meeting between the admins and the teachers, they tried to come up with different budget plans, but the majority were displeased with them. Since the budget crisis was already a serious issue, a few teachers gave the idea to organize an activity where students and teachers could be given a chance to present a budget plan from each Section of each Grade. In this manner, the school administration will also get multiple budget plans and can make a final decision on the best one. If the budget plan gets approved and works, the school will award the section with a trophy for now.

Upon continuous insistence, the school administration agreed to the teacher's idea. Even though the budget cuts would heavily impact the academic and extracurricular position of the school, allowing the students and teachers to engage in such activity will increase the variety of budget plans they could implement for maintaining not only the reputation but also the standard of the Broad School.

Grades 8, 9, and 10 and their respective teachers could take part in the budget planning activity. The teachers were only allowed to share their perspectives with the students and point out any ideas they might not agree with. Other than that, most of the budget plans needed to be designed by the students only. Moreover, each section must have a student from the student government who would represent the budget plan to the administrators when ready. The plan that would cut down costs in a way that the ongoing or upcoming activities aren't postponed or cancelled would gain additional points.

The student government alerted the members from Grades 8, 9, and 10 and informed them of their responsibilities. The dedicated and enthusiastic members of the student government sought to aid the school in matters of difficulty. Their spirit was about to be tested when they were informed about the budget crisis and the budget planning activity. The budget cuts threatened both the factors, academic and extracurricular, which defined Broad School. To counter the crisis head-on, the student government made a plan to spread their diverse talents within the teams of different Grades.

Three students of the student government from three different grades will be representing their grades in the battle of the budget soon. Each student developed a think tank with their respective grade students and their teachers. The team collaboration encouraged all the teams to do their best and made the students from the student government lead their budget plans. Each grade leader demonstrated good leadership qualities such as actively listening to every one of the students so they couldn't miss any great ideas, effectively communicating the entire issue to the students and asking for their cooperation, and impressively making accurate and informed decisions.

The decisions the plan leaders made were not only going to balance the school's budget but also resolve any previous or current conflicts and shape the future of the Broad School. Join the plan leaders as they embark on a journey of highs and lows to design an efficient budget plan for their schools. Will it save the standard and reputation of the school?

The next day started with a shift in the Broad School, from being a school with a lively environment, active teaching surroundings, and a sense of unity to a school with doubt if it would maintain its standards and stand up to its name. The temporarily implemented budget plan shocks the students, teachers, and parents. As the day passes by, the tension about the school's budget increases, displaying a noticeable worry among the administrators.

The immediate impact of implementing such a budget plan was more visible throughout the entire school. The lively discussions of students had reduced drastically, and gossip was more common. Teachers weren't able to deliver the quality education as promised because of the budget limit from the Broad School. The majority of the extra-curricular activities were hosted by the student clubs. Unfortunately, they had to temporarily close as well.

The student government members couldn't withstand what was going on with the school. They organized another meeting to get updates about the budget plan and pushed the members from Grades 8, 9, and 10 to work harder. Not only did the student government push them, but the teachers now encouraged them to give their best as well, as the school needed a good budget plan.

The three leaders from each grade met up during the break and shared the budget plans. There were some occasions when two leaders would agree on something but one wouldn't and other occasions when two leaders would disagree on something but the other would agree on it. The budget crisis was making every part of the school worry about what was about to come.

After a lot of discussions and multiple meetings with the class teachers, a final budget plan was created. The plan was presented to the admins and the community members. The plan comprised numerous academic and extra-curricular activities based on their priorities and the budget each requires. This method of listing each activity sorted by the budget made it easier for everyone to assess and analyze. There were a few points on which either the admins or the community members disagreed. The representatives of the budget plan were asked to step out of the meeting room.

Just a moment later, they were asked to come back in. These students could see their teachers and community members smile while the admins had a serious look. The school had collectively decided to select the student's budget plan for the future. They couldn't hold their emotions back, so they hugged each other and were grateful for the time spent together.

The next day, the school announced that no financial issue or budget crisis was going on. This was an activity planned by the teachers and the administrators to equip the students with efficient decision-making skills. The news regarding the budget crisis was purposely spread among the students and throughout the school so the students from the student government could emerge strong and tackle this serious problem. The principal later announced that they were very pleased by the efforts of all class members from Grades 8 to 10 and the student government for encouraging the selected team leaders to give their best.

**** **** **** **** **** **** **** **** **** ****

How would you have reacted if you learned that the school had a big crisis but that was just made up for an activity? You might get angry, right? But let's look at the bright side: the school management and teachers wanted to equip the students with important decision-making skills that would help them in their lives ahead.

As I told you at the beginning, decision-making is a very important skill that cannot be overlooked if you are on the path to becoming a future leader. Just like decision-making, the skill of critical thinking is essential too. It is like a righteous guide that helps you in making decisions that will make the best sense. On some occasions, you have to analyze the situation, gather information according, and make a decision based on the information you have; with critical thinking skills, you can make a smart and well-thought-out decision with a better analysis.

My fellas, if you are stuck at some point, relax a bit and then think about the whole situation carefully. Your critical thinking will be your light in the dark, and it will guide the way out. During the guidance, you have to make the right decision, as critical thinking and decision making is related to each other.

As you read, the leaders from each grade took time to analyze every idea they got from their classmates and listed it down. After this, they had to collaborate to cut off some ideas and prioritize others as per their budget. Decision-making can be an individual and team skill as sometimes it's hard to make the right decisions alone, and with the help of other's perspectives, you can make a better and more effective choice.

Moreover, there were limited resources that the students and teachers could use. The use of limited resources and cancelling a few events encouraged the leaders to make decisions based on the available set of resources.

Chapter 9

Peaceful Pirates

My kind and innocent buddies, have you met people in your life who don't agree with your ideas or opinions? Or is there a moment when you and your friend were colouring the art together, but you liked colouring the object yellow, whereas he wanted to colour it orange? These types of occasions are called conflicts.

Conflict, in simpler words, is a disagreement between two people with different and opposite opinions. Sometimes, it can be an uncomfortable and annoying process that causes the majority of the children to be uneasy, angry, afraid, or other strong emotions. Conflict is a natural and frequently happening occasion in children's lives. It can happen over even the smallest things, such as toys, space, clothes, ideas, and many more.

To promote positive growth, you must learn how to resolve any sort of conflict. Just like learning from mistakes is a skill you should have, similarly, you should have the skill to resolve conflicts. Resolving conflicts also plays a vital role in the development of healthy friendship bonds. During conflicts, there are a bunch of children who become hopeless and freeze up.

You can dissolve the conflict through different methods: talking directly in a respectful manner, reaching a mutual agreement, and actively listening. Instead of misbehaving with the other person or getting in a physical fight, you should talk to him directly or schedule a talk with them. A respectful discussion will help resolve the conflict easily. Even if the person is a bit rude, you should be calm and respectful.

Secondly, you should acknowledge if you are wrong and apologize. After that, you can let the person know their mistake and reach a mutual agreement, even if it is sharing something or taking turns. You both will win in this situation.

Lastly, let the person speak, and your role is to actively listen to him. Actively listening to what he has to say will make him feel honoured, respected, and not left out. This alone can contribute to resolving the conflict, but after his side, you can share your side of the story.

If you aim to be a leader, you must know how to resolve conflicts. Am I not right? How will you dissolve a conflict between your team if you don't know conflict resolution? With the help of conflict resolution, you can strengthen your team bond, which will improve teamwork and make each member of the team satisfied. As time passes, your understanding of your team members will increase and it will develop trust that will help throughout your goal.

The Conflict Between Athletes

The town in which Broad School was located had a track and field stadium which wasn't used as the sport itself but more like a park for families. Everyone, including the elderly, kids, and women, would walk into the stadium early in the morning or at sunset. It was a wonderful place for families to hang out. Parents would race with their kids and make wonderful memories. Among those children who made such memories with their parents were Nicholas and Iris, students from Grade 8.

Nicholas and Iris were classmates but not friends because of frequent conflicts between them. Both were in deep love with the track and field stadium and converted their love for the stadium into love for being in the Broad School's athletes team. As last year's co-curricular activities were giving the best results, Broad School decided to put their sprinters and long-distance runners to the test as well.

Iris was a long-distance runner, whereas Nicholas was a sprinter. For an ordinary student, it might seem like a race, but for them, it was a serious battle. Those who knew about the difference between sprinters and long-distance runners could feel the tension beginning to rise between the two teams.

The school's racing event was about to be held in four days. The sprinters and long-distance runners had always been in practice, but to prepare themselves mentally, they decided to work on themselves harder than before. Iris was very dedicated to making her team proud, whereas Nicholas was looking forward to working for himself rather than his team. As Iris stepped on the school's indoor track to warm up her long-distance running, Nicholas blocked her path and told her to come back later as he was practising. Even though every student was allowed to use the indoor track at any time, Nicholas not allowing Iris to practice made her shocked and angry at the same time. This was the moment that triggered the conflict between the sprinters and long-distance runners.

After some confirmation from the sports coach, Iris confronted Nicholas and pointed out his rude behaviour. They both exchanged some heated arguments and accusations, which were stopped by their respective teams. The coach could see the conflict between both teams and decided to resolve the conflict in a unique but effective way.

Two days before the racing event, Coach called Nicholas and Iris individually at different times and told them that they weren't allowed to participate. Upon hearing this news, both reacted with a burst of emotions. Nicholas got angry, whereas Iris began to cry. Each of them tried to convince the coach to allow them to participate in the upcoming event. But the coach wasn't ready to hear them as he had something in mind.

Once they both had given up, the coach decided to give them the option of proving that they were good at resolving conflicts within the team and building the team's trust. Emotions had blurred their vision and none was able to realize why the coach gave them such a strange way of convincing him.

As the school used to organize extra classes related to developing leadership qualities, a session regarding team trust was going on the same day. Both Iris and Nicholas attended the class. They came across different activities that could build trust and understood the importance of respecting each team member's strengths. Nicholas realized that Iris was also in the same class, and so did Iris. The class teacher chose them to work in pairs and make a creative presentation. Both students were totally upset at the class teacher's choice, but they couldn't do anything and only collaborated.

As the session ended, Nicholas and Iris were declared to have made the best presentation of the class. They both were surprised yet still upset at their performance. Tiredness gave way to talk as they made their way across the difficult terrain. Iris talked about the psychological and physical difficulties of long-distance running, while Nicholas expressed his aspirations to smash school records in sprinting. It dawned on them that their enthusiasm for their sport was the same, even though their disciplines were different.

Their unexpected meeting with a fallen tree obstructing their progress on the trail marked a turning point. They collaborated to overcome the barrier, signifying the dismantling of obstacles between sprinters and long-distance runners in a magnificent demonstration of teamwork.

After their getaway, Nicholas and Iris returned to the track with a fresh perspective. Understanding that a balanced combination of endurance and speed was essential to the team's success, they conducted their practices with consideration for one another's requirements.

When the championships finally arrived, the track and field team at Broad School displayed a level of solidarity never seen before. In his events, Nicholas ran to victory, and Iris set new school records in long-distance running. Their combined accomplishment demonstrated the importance of dispute resolution for both individual development and the team's overall success.

Broad School had an exciting environment as they celebrated their accomplishments. Excitement was in the air in the gymnasium, which was decorated with banners and team colours, as ecstatic parents, instructors, and students gathered to celebrate their players' victories.

Standing side by side on the podium were Nicholas and Iris, both dressed in their team colours. Around their necks rested the weight of medals that gleamed in the light. An intense cooperation had sprung from the rivalry that had previously caused friction and strife.

Nicholas and Iris shared a look that said a thousand words in that moment of mutual triumph. The audience went wild with applause when they realized the two athletes had gone through a transformational journey in addition to their accomplishments. It was a triumph that spoke to principles of harmony, cooperation, and the power of working through differences rather than just being about athletics.

Mr. Henderson, the principal, came up to congratulate the athletes. Taking out his microphone, he spoke to the assembly, praising Nicholas and Iris for their incredible growth. He described their path from strife to friendship, highlighting the importance of their recently formed alliance in advancing the group's success as a whole.

**** **** **** **** **** **** **** **** **** ****

HAH! I knew it. The best thing on such occasions is to resolve the conflict as quickly as you can. No matter how aggressive a conflict is or is about to become, you must focus on resolving the conflict. The story of Nicholas and Iris shows each stage of conflict resolution beautifully.

Let us begin with the first step of conflict resolution. When Iris went to the indoor track while Nicholas was practising, he stopped her and triggered a conflict. A conflict that was further escalated due to his rude behaviour and Iris's over-reaction. Both the sprinters and long-distance runners realized the increased tension and hindrance in performance due to the conflict. With the help of the coach, Iris and Nicholas were able to identify the conflict, which is the first step towards conflict resolution.

Secondly, my young fellas, you should know how important it is to solve the conflict as it doesn't only affect you and the person you've conflict with but people around you as well. Just as we can see in the story, even though there was a conflict between Nicholas and Iris, losing a strong team member from each side reduced their confidence levels. The team's overall performance went down, and their spirit was beginning to weaken.

Thanks to the coach, Iris, and Nicholas understood that it was important to resolve the conflict between them to be in their respective teams. Classmates who weren't friends and got famous for conflict were forced to take part in team exercises and managed to come first. At this moment, they realized that their collaborative team efforts made them a more powerful duo.

As you can see, they had a common goal, and that motivated them to convert conflict into cooperation, and by the end, they transformed each other to be better and contribute to the success of their teams.

For my future leaders, conflict resolution is an essential leadership quality that should be instilled in you. As you know, leaders bring positive transformations in teams and strengthen the bond between team members, which is only possible if there are no conflicts. Leaders can foster a healthy environment for all the individuals on the team where everyone is valued, and there are no hard feelings between the teams.

Chapter 10
Heartful Heroes

You all know human beings go through different emotions throughout the entire day. Either happy, sad, angry, or any other powerful emotion, depending on what they went through. But do you understand what emotion is? I am sure that you people understand how it feels.

Emotions give everyone information about how a person feels at the moment and what the person wants or needs. In order to connect with other people, we should understand and respond to other people's emotions and support the people in the best way out there. By understanding other people's emotions, we can also express our care for them.

In the simplest words, an emotion can be defined as a person's inner feelings. If you can't tell how you feel, let me explain the different emotions a person feels based on common scenarios. Imagine you are building a castle with Lego, and you almost complete it, but then your friend or sibling destroys it either by removing a piece or kicking it. Now, you are experiencing either anger or frustration as you worked slowly and gradually to build it from the beginning.

Similarly, imagine it's your birthday, and you have been very excited to celebrate it, but no one remembers. You are now feeling a bit sad because of no celebrations, and just as you entered your room, a group of friends jumped at you and screamed, "HAPPY BIRTHDAY!" now your sadness will convert into happiness.

Lastly, you are with your cousins, and now it's late at night, and they are about to leave. You insisted they stay, but they can't because of school. Now, the emotion you are experiencing is sadness because you want to have more fun, but they have to leave.

My strong companions, the power to understand and manage your emotions, along with the emotions of people around you, is known as emotional intelligence. You can also consider it a superpower for humans. Remember, healthy and positive emotions can shape your life and influence people around you as well.

Engaging in verbal communication with your friends and families will develop a strong trust bond between you and them. You will be better at expressing your heart, and so will they. At the same time, once you get used to understanding their emotions, you will respect them too, and how they feel.

The feeling of mutual understanding between the teams is essential for team collaboration, and it can help in developing new leadership qualities. People with emotional intelligence develop positive bonds, pay more attention in classes and to their surroundings, and are more active in school, too.

However, there are also negative emotions that should be managed and kept in check, as they can have the opposite effect of positive emotions. If you are angry, lonely, sad, or experiencing any other negative emotion, it can be difficult. I can understand, but at that moment, you have to be calm and patient. Negative emotions can lower your self-esteem and confidence levels, and eventually, you begin to dislike yourself. We don't want that, do we?

I want you to stay strong, focus on positive emotions, enjoy your positive moments, raise your self-esteem, and boost your confidence levels. Life can have its ups and downs. When you come across any downfall, don't lose hope, and don't fall behind. And if there are ups, be grateful for all the positive feelings. We can use the superpower of emotional intelligence by taking a few moments every day, thinking about what makes us happy, and paying attention to what is happening currently. Even if it is like feeling the warmth of the sun or hearing birds chirping, we should practice gratitude and make our hearts feel happier than ever.

The Positivity Club

After completing the class on mental health awareness, Ms. Janet, an aged English teacher, known for her kindness, affection, and passion, made the decision to start a positivity club. During her last class, she could see several students who were quite interested in the topic and some who showed a look as if they needed some help too. Doubt and insecurity usually clouded students who were seeking to improve their mental health. When she tried to reach out to those students, she didn't receive any positive response.

In Ms. Janet's classroom, students from diverse backgrounds and cultures, some from loud urban cities and some from old rural areas are present. Each student brought a unique set of visions and perspectives to the class. Their liveliness and class participation enhanced the learning experience of the entire class. One day, when she entered her classroom, she could see her students expressing different emotions on their faces. Some students showed sadness, while others displayed excitement for the class. Before she started teaching, she asked each student to come up to the front and share how they were feeling and why they were feeling that specific moment. This activity created a burst of excitement among students and altered the atmosphere of the class.

Students came up to the stage and, one by one started sharing their emotions with the class. As Ms. Janet was an experienced senior teacher, she was confident about the understanding of her student's emotions. She was curious, out of care, to hear students who were feeling negative emotions. A few students were happy about bringing tasty lunches, some about meeting their school friends, and others about getting stars on their homework. Now came the turn of students who didn't seem happy. A bunch of students got scolded by their parents early in the morning, which made them upset. Some forgot to bring their lunch, and the remaining 2 students were angry as they had a fight between them.

Upon hearing each of her students about their feelings and why they were feeling a certain way, Ms. Janet decided to teach them a topic of emotional intelligence. She instructed the students to calm down and allow her to speak.

"So, you all know what emotions are?" asked Ms. Janet in a soft tone.

"YES!" students said collectively.

"Are you emotionally intelligent?" Ms. Janet smiled as she asked because she thought it would be the new topic of today's class.

The entire class went silent, and the teacher asked the same question, but no one responded. As she was about to continue speaking by talking about emotional intelligence, a student raised his hand. The teacher stopped and asked the student to proceed.

"What is emotional intelligence?" asked a student out of curiosity.

Ms. Janet started by teaching students about emotions and then emotional intelligence. She explained how important it is to understand and manage emotions not only of yourself but others, too. The students thought to themselves, why is it necessary to understand other people's feelings and emotions? Just as they were about to ask their teacher this question, she had already begun answering the question.

"When you understand other people's emotions, you develop a strong and deeper connection with them and begin to empathize with them. As time passes by, you will communicate more freely and support them at difficult times. When you care and support people around you, it will create a caring atmosphere for everyone. In the end, when you are in need, the same people you understood will be your support.", told Ms. Janet, while she looked into every student's eyes and saw a spark in them.

The discussion related to emotional intelligence had already changed the class atmosphere. It began a series of fresh gossip among friends and activities that would mould the minds of the students regarding understanding emotions in themselves and others.

This level of enthusiasm and spark regarding such a topic encouraged Ms. Janet to bring her idea of a positivity club into reality. She went to the principal to discuss her idea with him and shape it into reality. Her idea impressed the principal, and he supported the formation of a positivity club for students. The Broad School formed a positivity club under Ms. Janet's guidance. The purpose of the club was to create a kind and supportive community, promote kindness, mental health, and well-being, and fight negativity. She shared about the club with her students and got an unexpectedly sympathetic response. Only a day had passed by, and the response of the positivity club shocked Ms. Janet. There were more than 100 students who wanted to be a part of the club. The teacher wasn't able to hold her happiness inside. She asked the applicants to list down their names and sections, after which she welcomed each member of the newly formed club. The students were very excited to be under Ms. Janet's guidance, as she was one of the kindest teachers at the Broad School. Students were confident that this positivity club would be a success because of such an amazing teacher.

Unfortunately, nothing happened on the first day of the club, as Ms. Janet had to list down each member's name for herself. She was a little sad when she thought about the first day, as the response was good, but she wasn't able to begin the first day of the club with an unforgettable session.

When the school classes ended for the day, Ms. Janet slowly walked to her car. With a burst of mixed emotions revolving around her mind, she couldn't do anything except smile, hiding the sadness of not being able to do something on the first day of the Positivity Club. She drove her car carefully and reached home after an hour. When she came home, she had lunch and went straight to bed.

No matter how kind, pleasing, and lovely a teacher she was, she had a heart as well. She had a dream. She could see the number of club members increase by a huge amount the next day, and she was super happy about it. The dream also showed some fun activities that took place. Upon waking up, the first thing Ms. Janet did was to list down all the activities she could remember. She was excited for the next day at the positivity club. Listing down activities and ideas on how to improve the club further occupied the rest of her day.

The next day, when the classes ended, she could see her dream come true. More students were willing to be a part of the positivity club. She called out two students from the 10th grade and made them members of the management team. The new members were proud that Ms. Janet had selected them and aided her in registering the new students. Meanwhile, Ms. Janet wrote down on the whiteboard the activities that would take place based on the days of the week.

Monday: **Collaborative Art Activity**
Tuesday: **Random Acts of Kindness Challenge**
Wednesday: **Active Listening Circles**
Thursday: **Emotion Wheel Activity**
Friday: **Journaling Activity**

As it was Wednesday, Ms. Janet was about to organize active listening circles, but the never-ending registrations delayed the progress. As soon as the registrations ended, Ms Janet guided all the students to the football grounds and asked them to sit in a large circle with her in between. Around 60 students surrounded her. She cleared her throat and then spoke confidently and loudly about the introduction of active listening circles activity. Students asked different questions related to the activity, which Ms. Janet answered promptly. As a large circle was formed, and Ms. Janet didn't want to break it into smaller circles, she assigned group names to each student.

Each group is composed of 5 members. Every week, the groups would switch, with one group presenting while the others paid close attention. This was how the Positivity Club worked on Wednesdays. This organized approach gave each participant a specific opportunity to discuss their unique experiences or concerns in an inviting and favourable environment.

The first member would stand in the centre of the circle and gather their confidence to speak in front of the positivity club members. Some students started with trembling voices, whereas others were bold from the beginning. As they spoke, the other members would carefully listen and would develop empathy and understanding for the speaker. No judgments, no interruptions, only the formation of new bonds of trust and empathy between the students of the Broad School.

Upon finishing, the speaker would go back to their position in the circle and sit down. The second member of the group would replace their place in the centre and would continue to do the same thing. Ms. Janet assigned this activity to all the upcoming Wednesdays until all the students have gotten an opportunity to speak their side.

As the teacher assigned an Emotion Wheel activity on Thursday, the Positivity Club had a different setup on the next day. Students were asked to sit in an auditorium. The students saw the management team members bring a large spinning wheel to the front of the stage. Once placed in the centre, Ms Janet asked them to take their places and started explaining the activity to everyone. On the spinning wheel, she had listed a wide variety of emotions. She told the students that she would ask a student to come up to the front and spin this wheel, and whatever emotion the arrow points at would be the topic of Thursday's session.

Students had to describe what would trigger those emotions; it could be any scenario or event. They were also asked to share how they would manage that specific emotion. This was a unique yet interesting activity. On the first Thursday, after the Positivity Club formation, the spinning wheel stopped at the "anger" emotion. The students were very excited to speak about it, and their response pleased Ms. Janet. She asked a countable number of students to come up to the stage and share their opinions with the class. After this, she invited another bunch of students to tell them how to manage their emotions effectively. This activity opened up the minds of many students and taught them how they could channel their emotions properly. It was another day when the previous topic had to be continued in the next upcoming week.

Ms. Janet came home with a strong sense of accomplishment. She was very pleased to see the response of the Positivity Club during the last and current day. The positivity club became an additional source of motivation for her to go to school and be more active so she could make a lasting impression on students.

Friday had finally arrived, and the activity assigned to the Positivity Club was the Journaling Activity. However, unlike the previous days, which were filled with excitement and enthusiasm, the attendance of Positivity Club members was significantly less. Ms. Janet became concerned as she saw the empty chairs in the class. Even though it wasn't much of an issue, she felt slightly sad. With a kind and soft welcome, the teacher greeted her students who were present and thanked them for attending the journaling activity. The journaling activity was nothing exciting compared to before. It was more like an extra class in which Ms. Janet talked about the journaling purpose, benefits, and how-to guide. Students made sure that they applied the knowledge they obtained from the journaling activity day in their daily lives.

Ms. Janet didn't have a habit of this level of activeness, so she was looking forward to the weekend. She spent most of the weekend resting and thinking about how to manage the club efficiently. Monday was finally here; students eagerly waited for this day to participate in the collaborative art activity. Students mainly wanted to express their creativity using art. Ms. Janet and the newly formed club management helped distribute students to teams based on their strengths and weaknesses. Each group had students which balanced the overall characteristics of the team.

After asking all the club members about the art topics, they collectively came up with a decision to organize an art topic lucky draw each Monday. Basically, all students would write their favourite thing on a small piece of paper and put it in a large bowl. After shaking a bit, the teacher would pick one and announce it, and that would be the topic of the day. In this manner, the topics will be random and fair to everyone. This Monday's art topic was a vintage car, a topic which cheered only a few students. As the timer started, some students requested Ms Janet to draw her favourite vintage car too. Ms. Janet didn't have any car preferences, but she had lovely memories of her father's car. Upon grabbing the stationery and a paper, the students cheered her up, making her giggle. Another unforgettable day folded as the students collaborated with their respected teams and created amazing art pieces.

Personally, the teacher was keenly waiting for Tuesday's activity. An activity that would develop the hearts of students into softer ones and promote kindness throughout the campus. The new day started with the same routine, except this time, at the beginning of the classes, Ms Janet explained the purpose of this activity, asked students to do an act of kindness, and informed them by the end of the school classes. Students started panicking as they couldn't think of many ideas, but Ms. Janet calmed them and gave them a hint to eye daily life. Unfortunately, this time the response wasn't near the previous responses. The students were present, but they hadn't completed their tasks.

Students had their heads down when the teacher asked about their acts of kindness. The teacher assured them that it was alright and that they would get it done with no help. This encouraged the students to do better next time. Those who successfully did any act of kindness then shared it with the club, and Ms Janet further added how students should learn from these incidents. The day ended with students leaving for home with faces held high, full of enthusiasm, and high self-esteem, thanks to Ms. Janet. The activities continued even after Ms. Janet retired, and the students remembered her as the most caring and kindest teacher of the Broad School.

**** **** **** **** **** **** **** **** **** ****

What a sweet teacher Ms. Janet was. She cared about the students and their physical and mental well-being. She was the real "Heartful Hero" who was already transforming the lives of the present students and became the founder of a club that later transformed the lives of the current and future students, too. Introducing a club for the students was one of the most inspiring things she did for her students. Besides that, she set up a plan that highlighted the activity of the day, making the Positivity Club engaging and exciting for all the students, whether old or newly enrolled. My young children focus on what I am about to tell you closely. Let's break down Ms. Janet's weekly activity calendar and understand how it helped students.

Monday's activity was the collaborative art activity, in which students learned teamwork, collaboration, creativity, emotional expression and well-being, and mindfulness. Students had to work in groups, share their ideas, be as creative as they could, and even express their emotions through art. Through this activity, you can be in the present moment with no judgment and be mindful of yourself.

Tuesdays were about acts of kindness. By performing acts of kindness, students developed a better understanding of emotional intelligence. Each kind act made them happy and boosted their positive emotions for two main reasons: they felt good while doing the deed and realized that they were creating a positive, lasting effect on someone. Moreover, this habit fostered gratitude and sympathy within their hearts. Eventually, this results in better well-being and a stronger connection with the community.

A vital activity that would give a boost to expressing emotions and understanding others was Wednesday's active listening activity. This activity also covers the basic leadership qualities that we learned earlier. It promotes effective communication skills, as you have to gather confidence and speak up, sharing your moments from life. The remaining students will actively listen and develop a better understanding of the situation. This activity would also promote conflict resolution, as you will learn how to tackle conflicts positively.

Similarly, Thursday's emotion wheel activity helps in understanding emotions better, promoting emotional intelligence as a superpower. Students will comprehend a deeper understanding of emotions by listening to the unique experiences of students. It will instil a strong feeling of empathy in the students, making them kinder at heart and more compassionate.

Lastly, Friday's journaling activity helps students express themselves through the journaling medium. By documenting their emotions in a journal, students can reduce their stress and begin a journey of emotional healing. Writing down your thoughts and feelings in a journal can help you understand them. This will make you emotionally strong and give you control over your mental health. Expressing emotions in a safe environment leads to a greater sense of empowerment.

My energetic comrades, I know this might sound boring, but once you also do these activities, it will put you on the right track to becoming a leader. You will develop the characteristics naturally without forcing them onto you. Just like students remembered Ms. Janet, I would love to see you guys remember me when you are strong and inspiring leaders.

Part 2
Fruitful Activities for Little Leaders

Chapter 11

Mighty Minions
of Responsibility

My junior comrades, your parents might have told you multiple times to do your chores, maintain and tidy up your rooms, or water the plants. They expect you to do these types of tasks. Those tasks are your responsibilities, as you are expected to do them. Responsibilities pack a punch of transformative power that can influence your daily lives. Fulfilling your responsibilities nurtures confidence and boosts self-respect as you begin to notice your part in positively impacting the household. Everyone will start to respect you and trust you more often as you become a reliable person, and as you know, good leaders are always reliable.

If you are a responsible leader, your community will support you immensely. Taking responsibility for your actions not only polishes your leadership skills but also boosts your personal growth, and you will begin to inspire others. You will be successful and satisfied with your efforts and contribute towards a positive environment where everyone is honest about their goals and accountable for their actions. Such a community will always be successful because of the community residents' reliability, honesty, and accountability.

A character you should learn initially is a responsible attitude, even in the academic area, which is academics, and especially towards your personal possessions. Developing an accountable self is achieved by acquiring ownership of action and contributing to your personal development and success. Responsibility covers different aspects when it comes to academic activities; homework should be done before the deadline, attending classes actively, and seeking assistance where necessary. You are reasoned out to consider the need for self-determination and to have patience in learning. You should be confident enough to act as your own educational leader. This may include setting realistic goals, establishing a disciplined study routine, appreciating your own effort, and celebrating progress.

Taking care of your possessions also embraces cultivating something which is responsibility. Once you will understand the value associated with your assets it will become more obvious for you to take ownership and prove respect towards them. You have to go to your parents as soon as they will act responsibly in terms of organizing and managing their belongings. If they ask you to arrange the toys, or school supplies, or your clothes, all they're saying is that, in time, you're bound to learn that you have a sense of ownership of such possessions and also that they are objects of pride.

Already, this learning of consciousness is not only for material possessions. It also involves learning how to look after yourself physically and emotionally. This is based on activities like grooming self, regulation of feelings, and a healthy living lifestyle. Responsibility does not appear immediately but the development of the sense of responsibility creates a foundation for positive habits and decision making in your life throughout your life.

You can be a Might Minion of Responsibility, too! But you have to fulfil your responsibilities, as they will help you in building confidence in yourself, increase your self-esteem, and develop a feeling of being trusted, and valued.

Activities – Responsibility

My energetic comrades, you can learn more about responsibility and add its traits to your daily life by regularly doing the following activities. It will not only teach you responsibility but also equip you with the concept of the importance of accountability, consequences of actions, and responsibility in daily life for learning.

Before we start listing and discussing daily activities, we should learn that there are various types of responsibilities.

1. Personal Responsibility

It includes being in charge of your actions and behaviour. You have to own the decisions you make and be ready to accept any sort of consequences for those actions.

2. Social Responsibility

You must know the effect of your actions on society and other's well-being. It also encourages you to promote a positive change for the community.

3. Environmental Responsibility

You should remember that your actions can have an impact on the environment, and you should try to reduce any harm caused to the environment.

To be the next Mighty Minion of Responsibility, you should add these habits to your daily routine. It will help you learn core concepts of responsibility and put you on the right track to becoming the next leader of the future. By the end of these activities, you will begin to develop a lot of good and effective leadership qualities.

- **Age-appropriate chores:** Age-appropriate chores are essential for the growth of the child as they learn, for a sense of being, and responsibility as members of the family set-up. For children between 8 and 14 years, these chores present opportunities for the acquisition of useful life skills, as well as for offloading household activities onto parents and guardians. Parents and guardians assign younger children tasks such as making their bed, setting the table, and feeding pets. This helps them understand the value of contributing to family welfare and learn fundamental organizational and care skills. The ability to do one's laundry, clean one's bathroom, and help with dinner preparation becomes not only the learning of basic skills but also instils the notion of independence and autonomy. These tasks also provide valuable opportunities for children to learn about working together, managing their time, and taking responsibility. This sets a foundation for their future responsibilities, both at home and in other areas of life.

- **Babysitting:** This includes activities like watching out for a younger brother or sister, guiding them with homework, preparing snacks or meals, and protecting their well-being. Babysitting fosters responsible behaviour by making children first take care of another person's needs, schedule their time wisely, and make appropriate decisions when faced with difficult circumstances. It also promotes empathy, listening skills, and the ability to deal with emergencies in a cool-headed way.

- **Caring for a Pet:** If you own a pet, you have to take care of each and everything, from feeding it to bathing, cleaning, and even playing with it. Children learn a sense of responsibility from pet care by getting to their understanding of what it means to attend to the needs of another living creature regularly. They learn empathy and care-giving abilities as they learn to understand and meet the needs of their pet. The responsibility also comes from the direct results of the child's actions toward the pet.

- **Clean-up Race:** Let's transform the activity of cleaning into a fun competition in which children race against time or one another to clean up selected areas. The children might receive tasks such as sorting out toys, folding the linen, and cleaning the surfaces. Through the clean-up race, children learn responsibility and develop a sense of ownership and pride in a clean environment. As the children become used to the job, they become efficient, grab good relationships, work well independently, and can see things at young ages. We also understand the need to maintain shared spaces and that everyone must contribute to household activities.

- **The Money Game:** This game is filled with activities connected with money handling, for instance, budgeting, saving, and spending. But with children, the guided experimenting process of earning, budgeting, and spending play money within clear boundaries instils financial responsibility. They learn key financial skills, such as balancing needs and wants, setting goals, and evaluating the impact of spending decisions. Entrepreneur game promotes informed decision-making that is further founded on financial literacy.

- **Community Cleanup:** Cleanup in the community consists of assembling a group of volunteers who will remove litter and debris left off in public areas such as parks, beaches, or neighbourhoods. Participants commonly engage in trash cleaning, recycling items, and creating more appealing grounds. Community cleanups encourage environmental responsibility, civic pride, and a feeling of ownership by the community. They also educate participants about the need to manage their environment and personal influence on the environment.

- **Donating Clothes:** Making clothing donations includes collecting clean, used clothes and giving them to shelters, charities, or clothing drives locally. This kind of activity encourages decluttering and sustainability and also offers assistance to the needy populace, such as those who are homeless or otherwise poor. Through donating clothes to others, children learn about empathy, generosity, and charity. It also cultivates a spirit of thankfulness for one's possessions and makes one uphold grateful consumption habits.

- **Donating Toys to a Local Charity:** A toy donation drive needs to organize toy collection activities to collect used or new toys and donate them to local charities that assist children in need. This activity fosters generosity and compassion among children for they learn to picture the needs of others and distribute their stuff to others that are not as fortunate as them. It also imparts the importance of helping society and improving the lifestyle of people around you.

- **Kindness Challenge:** A kind challenge refers to an organized activity in which individuals engage in acts of kindness towards other people for a specific period of time. This can take the form of admiring another person, helping a neighbour, and even writing a note of thanks. The kindness challenges facilitate empathy, compassion, and positive relationships. This further motivates people to give their best to change the lives of people around them by being kind to them and teaching them a lesson of kindness.

- **Organizing a Fundraiser:** The process of organizing a fundraiser is thinking, planning, and executing an event or effort to raise funds for a specific cause or group. This could include bake sales, car washes, or charity auctions. Fundraising activities help youngsters acquire skills, including event planning, budgeting, marketing, and teamwork. They, too, represent generosity and social obligation since the company's participants seek to support an admirable cause and make a real improvement in society.

- **Energy-Saving Challenge:** Energy-saving challenge is a structured activity that might involve reducing the energy required from homes, schools, or communities to reduce the use of energy. People say to themselves that they aim to lower the consumption of energy using the appropriate practical but functional techniques such as reducing the brightness or shutting off the light, removing plugs and turning electronics off, getting energy-saving appliances, and not over-using the thermostats. The challenge offers individuals the opportunity to become more aware of the implications of energy conservation and, with that, the power to actively and creatively encounter sustainability.

- **Environmental Awareness Poster Contest:** A poster contest that promotes environmental awareness encourages competitors to design posters that enlighten people on various issues of concern in the environment and motivate them to take positive action. The participants can use their creativity to express visual messages covering issues like climate change, pollution, biodiversity loss, or sustainable practices. Through this contest, research is encouraged, as well as critical thinking and artistic expression in promoting environmental literacy goodwill within the community. When you receive a certificate of participation or secure a position, you will be pleased with your performance and add this to your achievements.

- **Environmental Storytelling:** Environmental storytelling is a practice of sharing stories, personal experiences, and narratives through different media like writing, spoken word art, and so forth that relate to environmental themes. The topics of environment conservation, wildlife protection issues, sustainable living, and even concerns about environmental justice can be addressed during this challenge. Environmental storytelling enhances empathy, connection, and environmental issues understanding while creating advocates of change through shared experiences in the stories.

- **Gardening:** Gardening activity is one of the most fun activities to do especially when it comes to growing plants, flowers, fruits, or vegetables indoors. The participants can establish gardens in their backyard, public plots, or just containers, even within the house. Gardening encourages environmental stewardship through direct interaction with nature, which leads to an understanding of ecosystems and biodiversity. As they engage, the participants get to know how to take care of plants, soil health maintenance, and water conservation, as well as the merits entailed in growing your food. Gardening also offers the chance to get physical, unwind, and exercise creativity while making for a greener world.

- **Recycling Crafts:** Recycling crafts involve reusing recyclable materials such as paper, plastic bottles, or cardboard to make artistic art projects and even utilitarian items. Participants can make sculptures, jewellery, or functional objects such as pencil holders and bird feeders. The art of recycling crafts has a lot to do with raising environmental consciousness and advocating for reusing materials or, at the least, reducing waste. They promote innovation, ingenuity, and frugal thinking, but at the same time, they create a mindset of sustainability.

Responsibility is a vital activity in terms of self-development and character formation at any stage. Performing duties that involve responsibility inculcates virtues such as accountability, honesty, and reliability. These activities not only help the students learn valuable life skills such as time management, organization, and problem-solving but also inculcate qualities like diligence, perseverance, and self-discipline. Life provides challenges, and in actively participating in responsibilities, individuals will develop the confidence and skills to navigate life effectively. Also, responsibility activities help people become more autonomous and self-sufficient as they learn to trust themselves in achieving objectives and fulfilling obligations.

Responsibility also creates trust and respect from others which contributes to positive relations, as well as mutual understanding in a personal or professional environment. In addition, such activities are usually linked to service for the community or society and stimulating social responsibility as well as preparing individuals for their duties in adulthood. Responsibility activities are crucial in the development of individuals' character as well as in teaching significant life skills and preparing them for career success among others.

Chapter **12**

Tiny Treasures of Tenderness

My young companions, you are about to start a journey to finding the tiny treasures of tenderness. You have successfully made it so far! To be honest, did you enjoy the responsibility activities? Aww, why not??? It might probably be because some activities might be boring, and you want to play video games rather than do a healthy activity. You should understand the journey of becoming a future leader might seem boring, but you are the one who can make it more fun and interesting for yourself. So buckle up; we are going to learn more lessons about leaders, leadership qualities, and activities that have the power to transform you into an effective and true leader.

Are you familiar with the term "Servant leadership"? Just imagine a leader who responds like your best friend or kind elder brother. That is what servant leadership stands for! Unlike a boss, servant leadership is actively listening to others and helping them wholeheartedly by acting just like superheroes who save the day because they help people in need. Servant leaders work towards creating an environment that makes everyone feel important and happy, like a captain, ensuring all teammates are doing good, physically and mentally, in an event.

Real leaders do not necessarily mean the people with the loudest voices or biggest muscles. They are like enormous elephants who use their power to lift others. Real leaders know that to be great is to show kindness and charity. They're like the brave knights who do not use their courage to fight but protect and serve other people. They demonstrate empathy by knowing and sympathizing with whoever comes into contact with them.

Think of kindness as a magical potion that makes the world happier. Small gestures such as giving a smile, thanking someone, or even helping someone carry their bags can generate waves of joy. These subtle gestures are like the seeds that one buries in the soil but which evolve and grow into big trees of joyousness and friendship. They demonstrate that sometimes even the simplest things make someone's day happier and happy as sunshine. Wouldn't that be a lovely feeling?

Let's pretend that you have a specific kind of glasses that is kindness glasses. These glasses allow you to see endless possibilities for being kind everywhere where you go! By paying attention to what people feel and require, you can use that to be kind to them. For instance, you notice when a friend looks sad and needs a hug or your help in class with homework. With your observation skills, you will find opportunities to brighten someone's day by being kind daily!

Since kindness requires little thought, one can easily compare it to activities like brushing teeth or tying shoestrings, which anyone can effortlessly do every day. You may begin by saying good morning with a smile, helping parents around the house, or sharing your toys with siblings/friends. It is just like having breakfast or praying before going to bed. When you indulge in this practice every day, it becomes a habit of being kind.

Picture a world where all people wear invisible kindness capes, secretly doing good and kind deeds but leaving a great impact! Someone is passing her kindness cape to you when they help out by doing something nice. Thanking and acknowledging their kindness is spreading the concept that acts of love bring on positive change. We all can be superheroes of kindness, saving the world and bringing light into it.

Activities – Servant Leadership & Kindness

Another bunch of activities that will make your learning fun! You must make sure that you actively take part in these activities, as it will help you develop the core concept of servant leadership and kindness. Kindness might have been a part of your life already, but you weren't familiar with servant leadership. Apart from learning about what servant leadership is, developing skills is very important for you to be a true leader and find the tiny treasure of tenderness.

> ➤ **Simon Says:** Simon Says is a classic children's game that's both fun and educational. In the game, one person, usually called "Simon," gives commands to the other players. They start each command with "Simon says." Players must only follow commands preceded by "Simon says." They should ignore any commands given without this phrase. The game helps children improve their listening skills. It also helps them pay attention to detail and follow instructions.

Additionally, it encourages physical activity and social interaction. It fosters creativity. Players take turns being "Simon." They come up with fun and imaginative commands for their friends to follow. It also teaches children the importance of paying attention and thinking. This activity is a fun game along with a valuable learning experience.

- ➢ **Conflict Resolution Via Role Play:** One of the best ways of learning conflict resolution is through role-play activities. Role play provides you with a safe place to work through tough situations. You might need to act them out for conflict resolution. After dealing with the conflict, you can think of other ways to resolve it. In this way, you will learn different ways to resolve conflicts between team members. You will become an effective, true, and serving leader. Great scenarios to role-play include resolving conflict with a bully, fixing a friendship after a fight, etc.

- ➢ **Feelings Detective**: The Feelings Detective game is an engaging activity. It is designed to help children explore and understand emotions. In this game, players take on the role of "detectives". Their task is to identify and read various feelings expressed by others. Players can play the game in different ways. For example, role-playing scenarios, picture cards showing emotions, or storytelling prompts. In the prompts, players guess the emotions of characters in a story. The game encourages players to pay attention to facial expressions. They should also watch body language and listen to verbal cues. This helps them determine how others are feeling. Children who actively participate in this game learn to understand and identify emotions while gaining empathy and improving their communication abilities. The Feelings Detective game not only makes learning about emotions enjoyable and interactive, but it also gives children a secure environment to express and explore others' feelings and experiences.

- ➢ **Feedback Seeking:** You can play Feedback Olympics by making different teams. Teams will compete in fun challenges focused on giving and receiving constructive feedback. This can involve role-playing scenarios, creating feedback sandwiches, or writing anonymous compliments. This activity goes beyond simply giving feedback. It's about creating a supportive environment where everyone feels heard and valued. Participants practice giving and receiving constructive feedback through playful competition. They do so in a kind and respectful manner. Helping others improve demonstrates servant leadership. It prioritizes the team's growth over personal gain.

- ➢ **Gratitude Letter Exchange:** Unlike Feedback Olympics, you don't have to make teams in Gratitude Letter Exchange. Classmates write heartfelt letters to thank their fellow buddies. They write anonymously and express gratitude for their buddy's actions, qualities, or contributions. Letters are revealed and discussed, fostering appreciation and connection. This heartwarming activity cultivates an appreciation for each other's contributions. Writing thoughtful letters expresses gratitude for someone's actions or qualities. It fosters a sense of connection and belonging. It's a small gesture that can have a big impact, reminding everyone of the value they bring to the team. This act of kindness exemplifies servant leadership. It recognizes and appreciates the individual contributions that make the whole team successful.

- ➢ **Mentorship Relay Race:** Students are paired with mentees. You can also team up with your favourite teacher. They complete "knowledge-sharing stations" together. They tackle tasks, offer guidance, and learn from each other's strengths. This unique activity pairs experienced team members with those seeking guidance. It creates a dynamic knowledge-sharing experience. Participants learn from each other's strengths and perspectives. This fosters a collaborative and supportive environment. Experienced team members embody servant leadership. They invest time and effort in mentoring others and helping others to grow and develop their skills.

- ➢ **Escape Room:** Who doesn't enjoy problem-solving games, in this case, escape room? The escape room is one of the best and most enjoyable activities among friends. It will enhance your critical thinking abilities and more. You can play it alone or with a group. Teams collaborate to read clues, solve puzzles, and escape a themed chamber within a time frame. Collaboration, communication, and problem-solving abilities are critical to success. This collaborative task demands teamwork, communication, and problem-solving abilities. The participants work together to overcome obstacles and leave the room. They learn to trust and depend on one another's strengths. This common experience develops feelings of connection and togetherness. It exemplifies servant leadership by putting the team's success before individual accomplishments.

> **Team Cooking Challenge:** The difficulty level of team challenges, like team cooking challenges, totally depends on team collaboration and individual skills. Real success is displayed when you are planning, preparing, and presenting a unique yet tasty dish meanwhile teaming up with others. This involves distributing tasks, actively communicating, and acknowledging and appreciating each other's contributions. This activity combines creativity, collaboration, and fun. This project combines three major factors: creativity, teamwork, and enjoyment. Teams work together to create a tasty dinner. They learn to delegate duties, communicate efficiently, and value one another's efforts. Cooking and sharing meals promotes connection and community. It exemplifies servant leadership by focusing on the team's well-being and happiness.

> **Personal Development Talent Show:** In the talent show, students can easily show off their talents of any kind and favourite hobbies. They may sing, dance, or demonstrate a skill they have learned. The emphasis is on personal development and praising one another's abilities. This unique platform allows individuals to showcase their talents and passions. It's a supportive environment. This activity fosters a culture of continuous learning and development. It does so by celebrating each other's strengths and encouraging personal growth. This act of encouragement exemplifies servant leadership. It empowers individuals to reach their full potential.

> **Board Game with Self-Reflection Twist:** Teams play a modified board game. Choices trigger self-reflection discussions about their actions and values. This leads to self-reflection and an understanding of leadership styles. This activity adds introspection to traditional board games. It prompts participants to reflect on their actions and values. Participants gain valuable insights into themselves and their leadership styles. They do this by discussing their choices and their impact on the game. Self-reflection is a cornerstone of servant leadership. It encourages continuous improvement and growth.

> **Outdoor Activities:** Engaging in outdoor activities is the best way to develop and shine leadership qualities. Teams engage in activities like hiking, camping, or volunteering in nature. Shared experiences build trust, communication, and teamwork. They help promote a sense of belonging and respect for the outdoors. Outdoor activities like hiking, camping, or helping in nature can help foster trust, communication, and teamwork among participants. It's a cheerful and relaxing atmosphere. Helping each other overcome challenges fosters a sense of connection. Appreciating the beauty of nature also fosters togetherness. This act of shared experience exemplifies servant leadership. It prioritizes the team's well-being and creates a positive, supportive environment.

To sum up, it is not a choice to be a servant and kind leader, but a necessity for true and effective leadership. Being kind, servant, and compassionate are a few qualities among the essence of becoming a true leader. When you are emphatic, compassionate, and servant, you will understand and prioritize those who are in need. Eventually developing trust, and collaboration drives your community members toward greater success and positive impacts. As you might know, good leaders are very kind, they uplift others with either small or large acts of kindness. Leaders can create an unforgettable first impression if they show kind yet simple gestures. In an era of doubtfulness, learning these qualities provides a glimmer of hope and a road to a better future. As a result, let us aim to lead with modesty, serve with affection, and choose kindness on all occasions, for these are the deeds that will make us true leaders and leave an everlasting mark of positive change.

Chapter 13
Whiz Kids of Change

What a lovely journey it has been so far, my comrades! I am excited to have more thrilling adventures with you all. Let's add fun to our lives by enthusiastically doing the activities mentioned in each chapter now. Before we become the new whiz kids of change, we should learn about more leadership qualities. In this chapter, the leadership quality we will focus on is adaptability. In simpler words, adaptability means how a person can easily adjust to new situations or a change in life. As you might know, life has its ups and downs, if you can adjust to the changing conditions or environments, you are adaptable. A true leader has to adapt quickly to new and unfamiliar situations. Leader has to effectively manage change, and guide their teams to achieve the shared goals. To have continuous growth, leaders should be adaptable.

Remember my future leaders, you will come across multiple things in life, and change is a thing that might hurt you initially. But as time passes by, it will be easier as you practice. You can tackle any sort of difficulty related to change by considering it a new adventure. Start by welcoming change, followed by being excited for the unknown and new experiences. This will develop a feeling of joy and excitement to discover the unknown.

For a child of your age, you might have come across many new experiences, and yet there are more to come in the future too. It is equally important to understand why new experiences are a must in your life. New experiences improve your critical thinking and you can figure things out better than you usually do as you've been through that stage. Once you start to figure things out and tackle the problems, your self-esteem rises and you are braver and more confident. This eventually makes your new experience a learning adventure that you should be excited about.

To understand these better, new experiences are just like different kinds of snacks. Some are spicy, some are sweet and the remaining are salty. After having these snacks, you will learn more about two things; the new experience and details about the snack. Let's dive more into different activities that will help you be more adaptable and make you an effective and true leader.

Activities – Adaptability

- ❖ **Art and Creativity:** Making art and doing creative activities gives children an avenue to express themselves as well as accept changes through the activities of trying out new things and opening up to new experiences. Let the kid experiment with different art methods or mediums including painting, colouring, sculpting, or collage. During the activity, explain the learning and growing process that every art project involves - from learning new techniques to uniquely expressing thoughts and feelings. Adaptability is fostered by art as children learn to embrace the creative process and adapt to unforeseen outcomes which may be mixing colors on a canvas or reshaping a sculpture. Furthermore, creative activity spreads happiness and transcends children through the adventure of sending their imagination into reality. Working collaboratively on art projects reinforces bonds with one's family as children happily reveal their art creations and spend quality time engaged in shared creative experiences.

- ❖ **Building Blocks:** Building blocks are way more fun than toys – they are instruments for nurturing imagination, problem-solving, flexibility, and adaptability in kids. Encourage a child to play with toy blocks that range from LEGO bricks to wooden blocks, or magnet tiles. You should learn about how each item can be placed to create a variety of structures, simple towers, and complex designs among them. Constructing with blocks promotes adaptability as the children engage in experimenting with various configurations and learning from trial and error. Play block, consequently, boosts happiness and enthusiasm as kids enjoy the process of maturing from ideation to implementation. Together families and friends working on construction projects enhance relationships. This is so because children cooperate and brainstorm solutions together thus creating bonds as they form memories.

- ❖ **Cook n Bake:** Cook n bake gives children the chance to experiment with various flavours, ingredients, and cooking methods, thereby developing flexibility and toughness in the kitchen. You could start with trying different recipes and different dishes, even from something simple like snacks up to complex meals. Examples of growth opportunities presented in each cooking/baking project include learning to make a particular type of cheese, bake a cake with missing ingredients, or create a unique dessert from scraps available in the kitchen. Cooking and baking train flexibility because you will learn to manage unexpected issues in the kitchen; for example, a child has to be adaptable as a result of an unexpected change in the recipe measurement or when a cooking mishap occurs. This also involves the activities of cooking and baking which involve discovering the happiness and excitement of making wonderful meals and delicacies to share with family and friends. Working together to prepare dinner and bake cookies facilitates bonding as kids focus on something brewing in the kitchen and learn to cherish a common meal as a family.

❖ **Gardening:** Gardening will give you a chance to interact with nature. They can learn about responsibility and the ever-changing beauty of growth and transformation. Motivate yourself to take part in gardening activities. For example, planting seeds, watering plants, and harvesting fruits and vegetables. You should analyze how plants react to various environmental factors. Gardening leads to persistence, commitment, and resilience to seasonal and climatic variations. Gardening promotes adaptability. Kids see the need to adjust their gardening techniques. They base these adjustments on their plants' requirements. At the same time, adjusting their techniques based on the environment's condition. Moreover, gardening activities develop joy and excitement. You will be able to see the seeds sprout like magic, flowers blossoming, and fruits forming. When you watch these moments, you will rush to your family and friends. You will share your gardening experiences. This will strengthen the relationship. You will work together to nurture your garden and create shared memories of plant growth.

❖ **Language Learning:** Learning new languages can give you access to new cultures, life lessons, and ways to improve personally and professionally. You can start learning by using mobile phone apps, reading, and playing interactive games. Each language poses particular challenges when learned, and there are great opportunities for learning, from mastering vocabulary to understanding grammar and pronunciation. The process of learning a language enhances adaptability. Children learn to work with different language structures and adapt their elementary communication skills to interact with speakers of the target language. Additionally, using language learning creates happiness and excitement for children. They explore the beauty of new words and sentences and feel glee when they can speak in another language.

❖ **Music Camp:** Enrolling in music or dance camp offers you a platform for self-expression, creativity, and personal development; also, through adaptability, resilience is built. In the beginning, do your research on all musical instruments, genres, and dance styles, from piano to ballet, or hip-hop. Understand ways through which each piece offers an avenue for development and education; from perfecting the beats and motions to demonstrating emotions and thoughts through performance. Music and dance teach adaptation as children learn to synchronize their movements during changes in pace and rhythm. Also, music and dance provoke enjoyment and happiness as you will learn the joys of producing music and expressing yourself through dance. Sharing music performances and dance routines builds relationships when you display your talents and get to form bonds for having common artistic experiences.

❖ **Nature Exploration:** Nature exploration means diving into the world of nature whatever the place: a walk in a local park, a hike in the mountains, or a trip to the seaside. You should explore the nature around you starting with the smallest insects and up to the great landscape. Read how various species of plants and animals find ways to cope with the ever-changing seasons and surroundings and identify the features of each ecosystem. By going out and roaming nature a child can build adaptability by mastering how to make his way through differing landscapes and weather conditions while at the same time creating within him a sense of curiosity about and respect for the beauty of the natural universe. Furthermore, spending time with nature gives chances for you to reflect and grow personally through separating from technology and the environment. Sharing these experiences in front of family members and close friends enhances relationships and leaves memories of major efforts in the wilderness.

❖ **Outdoor Camping:** Outdoor camping is an activity full of adventures where a person is exposed to various situations allowing him/her to connect with nature, learn survival skills amongst other things, and adapt to different outdoor scenes. You should actively take part in camping trips. Even if it's in designated camps, national parks, or even the backyard. Look into how camping involves psychological and physical preparation for such activities as sleeping under the unfamiliar sky, setting up tents, making a campfire, cooking out in the open, etc. Outdoor camping nurtures adaptability since the children must cope with the various challenges they encounter while living outdoors from adjusting to living in a tent to improvising solutions to unknown problems. Apart from all of that, going camping makes children happy as they witness the beauty of starlit skies, hear the sounds of nature, and have the freedom to explore outdoors.

- ❖ **Storytelling:** You can immerse yourself in books and the process of telling stories to find new societies, people, and concepts, and you can learn about adaptability and flourishing. Look for a range of books containing various genres, including fiction and non-fiction, and biographies. You can read thoroughly and talk about how each story brings characters that face challenges and difficulties and they evolve. Reading and storytelling develop adaptability in children as they identify with the characters and learn to predict plots and unexpected turns found in the stories. Alongside reading and storytelling, it causes satisfaction and eagerness as they find themselves in the make-believe world and embark on thrilling journeys from within their very homes. Remembering favorite tales, and breaking their motifs and messages enhances ties as youth bond over mutual reading experiences and tell stories of them reading together that will linger on.

- ❖ **Science Experiments:** Performing scientific experiments at home gives you a chance to investigate the principles of science as well as to enhance critical thinking. You can try simple experiments with the stuff found at home, making volcanos out of the garage and performing some elementary chemistry experiments. This will help you learn how each science experiment offers possibilities for growth and learning, which include making observations and predictions, analysis of results, and drawing conclusions. Science experiments promote adaptability as you will find ways to change variables and experiment with different methods for achieving the intended outcomes. Also, science experiments give happiness and wonder as children see the marvels of nature and the fun of being scientists themselves. Sharing experiment results and agreeing on their effects builds trust when children cooperate with their relatives and friends to uncover the secrets of the Universe.

- ❖ **Sports Time:** Sporting and physical games provide opportunities to engage, get challenged, and develop emotional and physical attributes. Whether it's playing team sports such as soccer or basketball, or taking part in individual activities such as swimming or yoga, you should challenge yourself beyond your comfort zone and enjoy the benefits of active living. Explore how each sporting activity provides possibilities for learning and development, for example, gaining new skills or mastering challenges and disappointments. Sports instil adaptability as you will learn to adjust to evolving game situations and change tactics on the go. Furthermore, sports introduce teamwork and companionship, where you work together to realize a common goal, fostering friendships and relationships that last a lifetime.

- ❖ **Traveling:** Visiting new places will allow you to break out of the mould and see change as a challenge of excitement. No matter whether it's a different city, country, or continent, let yourself immerse in the local culture, cuisine, and customs. Talk about how each place offers unique obstacles and promises of growth, from getting around unknown streets to new tastes and foreign languages. Travelling promotes adaptability as kids get used to changing environments and situations, for instance, adapting to differing climates or learning to function in public transport infrastructure. Besides, experiencing different cultures and traditions extends your horizons and develops a sense of empathy and understanding for people of different origins. Travelling together with family or friends builds relationships and lets you make amazing memories of discovering new places.

- ❖ **Volunteering and Community Service:** Volunteering and involvement in community development activities will give you a platform to contribute to the betterment of your communities. At the same time, you are also being taught the qualities of adaptability and empathy. You should join positive volunteer work like serving in a homeless shelter, cleaning public parks, or a visit to older people in a nursing home. It will help you understand how each volunteer project presents an opportunity for growth and learning, from developing empathy and compassion for others to learning how to adapt to different social situations and societies. Volunteerism develops adaptability in children. You will experience diverse community settings and interact with people from different backgrounds and ways of life. Further, community service motivates happiness and enthusiasm. Children get the feeling of impacting other people's lives. Talking about volunteer experiences with family and friends enhances relationships. You will become united by acts of kindness and have fond memories of giving back.

In today's world, it is crucial to emphasize the significance of being an adaptable leader. Leaders who consider change as an adventure, instead of a challenge, can navigate doubt with resilience and creativity. These moments of change and adaptation offer a chance for growth and innovation. Leaders guide their teams through tough times. They approach change with an open mind and a willingness to learn. This also encourages a culture of always striving to get better and moving forward. Therefore, let's embrace change as an adventure. Accept it as a driving force behind your professional and personal development. Assist people around us and ourselves in reaching greater levels of satisfaction and accomplishment.

Chapter **14**

Speakshine Stars

Public speaking is exactly like a superhero with words! It is the exact moment when you stand in front of an audience ignoring its size, and you speak clearly and loudly sharing something wonderful or significant. As a superhero who saves the world using powers, you are the one who will carry the words to boost the spirit, inspire, and educate the audience. It's an opportunity for you to not only shine, like a star on stage but also to show the world your leadership qualities and talents that make you different from the billions of people who exist. Double check, your confidence cape is on and your power words are ready to go. Let's be the next Speakshine star!

Every child owns a speaking magic, a combination of traits, and experiences, and is born with talents that make up the capability of good public speaking skills. Some will just appear energetic and smooth-talking as if they were born that way, which will raise their audience's charisma and enthusiasm. Others may have this power of words, when they speak they create lively imaginations which people will remember. While some children are very effective and expressive, others can impress the listeners by winning over them with their sparkling humour and kind nature. Every time a child speaks, the magic that is hidden within them is a reflection of their leadership qualities, a capability that allows them to express who they truly are and do so with commitment and hard work. You will find your inner strength and confidence by walking down the path of effective communication and self-development.

When a speech is cast with the right words, it is like a spell that casts the minds and the hearts to be moved. Each word is but a brick in the larger building, the selection of which is incredibly hard; integrated in the right order, these bricks form a collection of emotions, ideas, and inspiration. If a leader uses strong words to paint bright pictures into the minds of their audience, they can fully immerse the audience in their world and touch their souls. Public speaking skills help free those around us from their worries and enable them to experience happiness or sadness through the words we hear. Even after the speech is over, it leaves a long-lasting image on people's minds and shapes how they think. If you are a good public speaker, your words will be powerful to move people's hearts and positively change their lives.

My energetic youngsters, I want to inform you about the common fears of public speaking so that you can relate to them and overcome them together. You might have felt a bit scared or nervous when you were standing on the stage and speaking in front of a small audience. If you didn't experience such a feeling, that's great! For those who did, this is called fear of public speaking. Just like this fear, there are other fears too such as what will happen if you forget what you memorized and you don't know what to say. This fear is known as fear of embarrassment. Well, you shouldn't worry this much, everyone feels this way at some point. Take a big deep breath, practice your public speaking skills through different games or activities, and believe in yourself.

As we've learned together effective communication is one of the most important leadership qualities, that can be used to understand, guide, and unite people. It helps in creating a link between the leader and his team, impacting decisions, and encouraging healthy change. Similarly, public speaking is a significant quality needed to be an effective, inspiring, and true leader. My young companions make sure you go through each activity and implement it in your daily lives as it will help you a lot.

Activities – Public Speaking

- ✓ **A Different Conclusion:** In this activity, you will step into a realm where common stories become surprising with the help of different conclusions. How about a case study, a conversation around well-known stories or events, and then asking yourself the question: how to rewrite the story so it has a different conclusion? In this exercise, you will collectively with group members start exploring a list of different outcomes that will present the stories previously like never pictured before. The young audience is absorbed in the collective creation of a new story. This activity promotes teamwork and encourages a vision that may be humbler and more unique than common tales can be. A new world of possibilities is opened and the process is followed with excited discussion among the group members. Through the use of original endings that are surprising, practical, and stir a participant's imagination, not only do they become good storytellers, but also more creative professionals. In "A Different Conclusion", the characters don't just solve a mystery, but show how the power of different conclusions and our unlimited imaginations can come together and unleash endless options.

✓ **A False Vacation:** Think of your most cherished dream vacation place–the place where you find comfort, peace of mind, and freedom from homework or upcoming test burdens. Now imagine a scenario where you need to explain and convince people to choose it as their vacation spot too. You will then have to be confident in yourself and share why you think it is the ideal spot for vacation even if you haven't visited the place. It might not be an easy task to convince someone to go to Disneyland, but you can give it a try as it will be a learning experience for you. This activity can turn into a playground for storytelling expertise by encouraging participants to express their thoughts fully and compose a captivating story that manages to capture the imagination of the audience. The audience might ask you a cyclone of questions, but you have to answer them emotionally, turning new details into attractive stories. In addition to developing storytelling and public speaking skills, the activity allows you to become emotionally open to the unpredictable.

✓ **Construct a Meaning:** Get ready to be a part of a memorable trip full of laughter this amusing activity will lead us to. We divide students into small groups and give them the task, of untangling a mystery by figuring out a reasonable explanation. It's a blend of craziness that has got the audience laughing until they gasp for air and then scratching their heads and refreshing their thoughts. By participating in such activity, one gets clear knowledge of the influence of powerful words in a speech by shaping one's imagination and choosing colourful but true phrases to present their understanding to others. Hence, be ready as you jump in the playground of your imagination, and lose yourself in the merry-land of nonsense punctuation. Everyone would be laughing, while you will be sharpening your speech and ability to think outside the box.

✓ **Extempore:** In literal meanings, extempore means to be done without preparation. Similarly, this exercise is about public speaking without any preparation. This type of activity usually scares you because of lack of preparation, but you don't have to be afraid as you now have a helping hand. Engaging in a thrilling experience also called time-less speaking, where you're handed a topic on the spot and asked to speak for a specific duration without any notice is shocking. It is the one obstacle in which you learn to adapt and express your ideas while you are publicly speaking to persuade your audience more effectively. Public speaking without preparation not only makes you a good improviser but also helps you master arranging ideas effectively when under the pressure of time–this is a priceless skill that true leaders desire to obtain. As long as you control breathing and gestures and confidently attract the audience with on-the-spot interesting speech, an extempore will be a friend you use everywhere.

✓ **One Lie and Two Truths:** The mere act of truth-telling does not make one confident. Rather, it is through the development of trust in oneself that one can create the story, whether based on reality or imagined. Each member of the group takes their turn to share three statements about themselves: two of them are the truth and the remaining one is a lie. One by one, everyone speaks up confidently about themselves, meanwhile, the others actively listen and analyze their short speeches. The activity is not only about guessing who tells the lie but also about shaping the dramatic story which leaves the viewers doubt if they are pointing out the lie or the truth, polishing the art of making up stories. Moreover, it also helps in improving critical thinking and observation skills which will help you become an active listener and such skilled presenter who can confidently convey the message.

✓ **Prattle on about a Subject You Dislike:** They say there are two things people love to talk about: things they love and things they dislike or hate. At the start of this activity, the class members shall work on an argument in which they shall talk about a subject they don't like or against which they agree. Whether it's against the opinion of the audience, public speaking is a form of training where individuals must find creative ways to form strong arguments, even when their personal thoughts may be against the topic of discussion. It helps to build up the students' persuasive speaking skills as well as to increase their empathy and understanding. This gives chance to explore multiple viewpoints and even enables them to engage with the other sides. Overall, this activity improves their understanding of complex issues and helps them to have the ability to communicate efficiently across differences.

- ✓ **Storytelling Using Pictures:** Get ready to be a part of the storytelling activity where you will use your creativity and imagination to create a story based on the given pictures. The class is told that a sequence of pictures, each of which could twist the events into another amazing story, is in front of them. Embrace the textures, colours, and mysterious calmness of the picture, as you dive into a magical realm of creative imagination. You will attract them into your story created by the sparks of your imagination. That's a fantastic way to both shine forth and inspire the creativity and your way of thinking of participants while telling a story. As time passes by, you are given a chance to give life to a fascinating character, examine difficult areas, and determine the plot of the storyline that is based on imagination and curiosity. You'll be guided into the world that provides hints allowing your inner artistic world to explore this ability as you express yourself through storytelling. Storytelling using pictures is the secret to learning public speaking effectively and it is one of the must-have tools that every leader would want to possess in the area of public speaking skills.

- ✓ **Study the Experts:** Whether it is sitting down with popcorn and a notepad to listen to the speeches of your role models or speech giants such as Martin Luther King Jr. or Oprah Winfrey, you can learn a great deal about the act of public speaking effectively. In this activity, you are not just a silent viewer; you are rather someone who understands and learns every single aspect of their public speaking skill–starting from their confident posture to the sound of their voice, up to the strategic pauses that they used to make their speech clearer to the gestures chosen which are used to emphasize their message. It is similar to being a detective, searching for pieces of evidence that will help you solve the mystery of how to make a speech that grabs the attention of the audience. Being with the public speaking masters, you're not only learning the best but also you will feel their legacy and see speech that will even inspire you to ultimately transform your skills.

- ✓ **Super Spies:** Doesn't it sound like an interesting activity? Imagine an entertaining yet learning activity where cleverness is one of the aspects of the game. In this activity, students, act as spy teams and find themselves placed on amazing missions that present a variety of challenges they must work together on. They are assigned to different teams and presented with the greatest mystery they've ever witnessed or the riskiest mission to unlock. Everyone plays a part in the story, the detective, the spy, and the informant, each one using their special skills to follow clues, untangle suspects' pasts, and stop the enemy. With the milliseconds ticking away and the tension rising slowly, teamwork and communication become the main point for attaining the shared goal. At this moment you have to confidently make up a story and convince other players to believe your story. This game adds strength to your speech and makes you more confident in public speaking.

- ✓ **Talk Pointlessly:** The English language alone presents not one but countless resources to help us grow our vocabulary. Picture this in your mind: someone gave you a random topic on something so silly, like how garden monsters are leading secret lives, and they start you off with a two-minute clock and tell you shouldn't make any sense ever during that time. Here is a lifesaving reminder that the joy is not to strain or worry about how you present yourself but to speak pointlessly and enjoy the foolishness you are in between. Imagine having a serious discussion about the issues of a garden monster or random reasons to answer why people crave ice cream in a way that is not humorous. This activity is not only an entertaining one but also about improving your ability to think and improvise while you have to make a quick speech in a real-life situation as it is significant for art. One way of doing this is by accepting the silly things that may accompany it, and through this, you are accessing your creativity and polishing your public speaking skills. This leads you to be a speaker that is adaptable and fun for others to listen to.

- ✓ **The Origin Story:** Take note that the activity "The Origin Story" will encourage you to think outside the box without limiting your imagination. If you ever found happiness in sharing stories about magical creations and supernatural lands, then you will love this activity as it is particularly for you. Whoever takes part in this activity will easily dive into a thrilling and innovative world where they create and unveil the origins of imaginary magical creations and supernatural lands. I want to believe that creating backstories for tiny objects is about bringing life to things that we take for granted and filling them with the energy of our imagination. The best part is that this exercise is truly rewarding and motivating; it awakens the fire of creativity and enhances the ability of the mind to imagine and visualize endless imaginary worlds. It becomes a journey for the participants of unwrapping the secrets of ordinary objects in fascinating ways while being more confident and improving their public speaking skills. The use of imagination and creativity prompts participants, in this exercise, to create original and captivating tales that astonish the curiosity of their audience by taking them to fantastical places.

✓ **Thirty Seconds Without Fillers:** Begin with this scenario: that is, consider just any normal sentence such as "Here are the benefits of yoga," and you're expected to talk for only thirty seconds without using unnecessary words like "um," "uh," or "like" as the fillers. Although the activity may appear straightforward, speaking continuously like this can be so challenging that even forcing you to just barely rely on these fillers won't do any good. This exercise finishes with the development of skills for more proper speech, by learning to think more over your wordings and say what you have to say with clarity and confidence. While you keenly focus on removing fill words, you not only hone your speaking skills but also improve your qualities as a speaker by becoming more reasonable. And that's exactly why filler words shouldn't be used in an argument: an unending series of "ums" and "uhs" is an obstacle on your path to public speaking excellence. So, by mastering the art of speaking without filler words, you're not only becoming a super-successful public speaker, but you are also gaining leadership qualities that will help you in your journey to be a future leader.

✓ **Tongue Twister:** Ah! Funny and tricky tongue twisters it is, where laughter is matched with angry and annoyed faces. It is in this activity where participants gradually dance around words that mix the flow of words by twisting the tongue. Imagine a room where people are rolling back and forth with the sounds of difficult tongue twisters that are surely made up to trip up the players at every step. Although the twister may not be the first to cross your mind, it does get into your mind throughout the day and acts as a skill-building component. This game belongs to the best pronunciation training where students are tasked to say each word of the phrase with attention, and without stumbling at any point at all. It's a funny and joyful activity which is, by the way, the one that exercises and develops both vocal skills and concentration. Words spoken during these mind-boggling sessions receive strong focus from participants who try to keep their attention and make the communication error-free even when it is necessary to deal with the most difficult speech forms. The giggles fade away while the tongues get back to their normal shape. By the time they finish the task, they are often more capable of putting their speech in order and comprehending the heart of the situation. You will learn that even those who can't deal with complicated words can still get a chance to succeed in everything they are doing.

These fun activities fully demonstrate the fascinating process of public speaking that children discover most effectively when they put into practice where they let their creativity and inspiration shine. Each activity is helpful and powerful in the path of discovering the incredible speaking magic within every child which is ready to be unleashed and appreciated for how it shapes them as little leaders. I have gone through all the exercises and I can assure apart from improving my communication skills, they have let me communicate better with people and they have brought my skills to a higher level too. They have also taught and helped me understand that the power of storytelling and communication cannot be less significant.

However, it is a fact that leaders have power in their words which makes them capture others through their inspiring speeches. It does not matter whether it is a motivating story, a convincing speech, or collaborative work; Leaders can achieve all their goals. The development of public speaking abilities in youngsters contributes to the learning of communication skills which, on the other hand, promotes the confidence to express thoughts, influencing change and, most importantly, positively impacting the world around us.

Moreover, if we think about the list of public speaking activities that are discussed above, it does look like public speaking is far more than simply owning the platform and delivering speeches – it is an entertaining trip to self-expression, imagination, and self-achievement. When taking up their speaking magic and using all the powers in their words, every child has the real and present opportunity to become a firm and thoughtful leader who is capable of guiding not only their small circles but the world at large. Hence, the view is full of possibilities whenever those future Leaders who are ready to truly shine, by optimizing their ability to speak, will emerge and shine.

Chapter 15

Coin Champion

Hey, future coin champs! Let's plunge into a world where we are surrounded by shiny coins and leaves that sparkle like a spell! Every cent is like a mysterious box in which lies a precious stone, and every dollar note is a small treasure wrapping a thousand tales. Because it is not just about acquiring things, but rather it's making sure to unlock several thrilling opportunities! Alright, shall we begin an exciting trip to learn more about the tremendous forces of money? Warm up your fingers to catch and count, sort coins, and even make your own money. In simple terms, money means a thing or any item that is usually used in exchange for goods and services like games, toys, or any other goods in particular.

To understand the basic concepts of finances let's imagine a magical kingdom and name it Moneyland, as it will help you remember the lesson. In this imaginary world, every coin and other form of money has different values. Budgeting is the art of drawing up a road map for spending money and putting plant seeds away for a time when you will be travelling again. Investing carefully is knowing how to take the right route, and giving is happiness for all of the kingdom. Through work, one unlocks new levels of achievement, and through investing, a seed of a future tree is planted. Working together, these concepts give you the ability to rule over your money, conquering the Moneyland with your new knowledge and understanding.

Living on a budget is all about determining how to get the best out of your survival adventure! Making a weekend plan right with your friends includes budgeting and knowing where to spend your money. It is no longer just about savings but careful planning and making good money spending. This is how being a captain of your ship while navigating the sea of money feels: making sure that your money can reach some exciting destinations while also saving some for future expenses.

Let's think of having a cupboard full of numerous toys, candies, and games ready to be enjoyed or played with. Taking time to learn how to manage and, most importantly, how to use effectively is similar to you being in charge of your pirate ship! It's a story about selecting those toys off the shelf that you are going to play with, and the snacks that you will be sharing with your friends. Moreover, it is a scenario that helps figure out when to save some treats for later. Preparation and usage of resources with care can make sure that you will simply do well with money handling. In easier words, it's like every day there is a chance of you being the smartest superhero in the world that shields you from being an empty wallet all the time!

Is it a lot to take in? My future little leaders you are currently on the right track! Slowly and gradually you will notice the huge difference between your old and new versions. As you might know, saving money is very important when you want to buy your favourite snack, gadget, or device. Learning to stop wasting money and saving small amounts is just like sowing some seeds in the garden whose fruits you will enjoy in the future. Saving is the process that involves storing some of the money you make and keeping it for the future, for example, someone putting his money inside a piggy bank or a savings account. When you save money, you are setting aside money for something really big and awesome like buying a new toy, travelling around and all sorts of other cool adventures, or even saving money for college one day! That is why, open your piggy bank and let the shiny coins be your magic wand– you will see the change reflected in your future life!

When we talk about money and saving, banks are the next topic on the list. Similar to magical wonders, a bank is a place where people keep their savings. Saving money in a bank doesn't matter if you need it immediately or in the future—it's more like a comfortable bed for money. A bank, however, does more than just hold your money; it also contributes to its growth. Banks create savings accounts so that you can store your money without any worries it getting stolen. Furthermore, banks lend out money, allowing people to buy cars, homes, or other precious stuff. Thus, whether you are saving for your next big adventure or have your eye on owning your own home, banks are a great place to turn to for assistance with managing your money and with the opportunity to turn your dreams into a reality.

In the following activities, you'll find yourself learning the secrets of managing money effectively, leading you in the footsteps of a true leader in the end. You will become more trained in managing your budget and the art of investing money. Each activity is focused on teaching you the necessary skills for being the king of the Moneyland. Whether you have just started savings and investments or you are already a pro at it, my goal is to give you the resources that will help you get where you want to be money-wise. Let us shift our minds for a moment in the direction of managing money which is another crucial quality for leadership!

Activities – Money Management

- ❖ **Ready, Set, Save:** "Ready, Set, Save!" is an interesting yet educational game that can be played with friends or siblings and you will enjoy it while also learning how to deal with money. To be able to play, each player will be given a specific amount of game money, which is equivalent to their savings. The players in turn use a die to move around the board which has various financial spaces representing different financial scenarios like being paid for chores at home, getting an allowance, being confronted by a sudden expense, or when they need to decide on expenditure. At the end of the game, players will face the same situation as in real life. They will have to decide where to put the money, whether it will be saved in case of emergency, will be used properly, or will be invested in an enterprise that has been already invented. The game challenges vacation thought processes and planning as players face financial difficulties and try to build savings. This game equips the children with important basic financial skills like budgeting, saving, making rational spending choices, and absorbing the consequences of decisions in a fun way thus setting a way for later well-informed financial opportunities in the future.

- ❖ **A trip to the grocery store:** This activity is information-rich and also allows families to teach about budgeting to children without boring lessons. The activity of grocery shopping together can be a great parent and kid activity. Before going grocery shopping, you should discuss with your family the size of the budget and which items need to be selected first keeping the budget amount in mind. While shopping, you will help in building a shopping list that is related to the household needs that do not make a mess of your budget. While you're in the aisle with them, ask them to do price comparisons, take a look at sales items or discounts, and also, let them know that their decisions should be made taking into account the value and the necessity of each product. Your parents can provide you with money to spend or include you in paying for certain products at the checkout counter. Once the trip comes to an end, you need to discuss the grocery shopping experience together showing the choices made and applying the lessons you learned. This activity helps in budget creation and a smart buying approach.

- ❖ **Budget-Friendly Cooking:** An exciting, fun, and social activity with friends that teaches them not only money management but also learning while having fun in the kitchen. The fact that participants will decide what amount of money in total will be taken off their budgets could be either a dinner party with all the homemade delicacies or a casual get-together. The expenditure has to include the base ingredient and any other items that would be needed for cooking. You and your buddies can then think through this budgeting issue and design a menu that fits into it by choosing recipes that are cheap though at the same time delicious and buying only pocket-friendly ingredients. There are so many things to be learned during the cooking process, such as shopping for fresh groceries to stretch a food budget which is possible by saving on generic brands or by buying in large quantities. If they succeed and the food looks good, friends can sit down together to savour the scrumptious dishes made from the cheap ingredients they purchased and discuss the vital things they have learned about smart spending and the importance of saving money. The students engage in this activity all while they learn the importance of teamwork in the cooking field, practical spending skills as well as budgeting.

- ❖ **Setting Up Lemonade Stand:** A simple yet thrilling game that allows children to learn practical knowledge in money management. You have to set up the equipment, like tables, chairs, cups, pitchers, lemonade mixes, and signs. After picking a spot that would be hard for people to miss like their neighborhood street corner or the local park, you can now position your stand there. At the end of the day, you can be a cash handler who attends to customers, handle money, and maintain records of earnings. The activity, among other things, is geared toward providing young students with hands-on experience in budgeting and practical learning as they see the need to price the ingredients to cater to their expenses and make a profit while also learning the benefits of saving part of their profit for future investment. Ultimately, this activity "Lemonade Stand" provides amusement and passion while at the same time leaving unforgettable memories on which children will be able to draw and apply in a variety of situations.

- ❖ **Money Management Board Games:** Many board games have their cash under the unique role of a banker. The most popular board game everyone has heard of is Monopoly. Board games such as Monopoly not only present a fascinating and educational way of understanding money management concepts but also give loyal players a memorable experience of having fun and spending time with friends and family. The game has been set up in such a way that players can choose to buy or trade from the given financial scenarios, managing their money and making decisions that ultimately determine how they spend the wealth they possess. You along with other players will be in situations in which the players will be able to understand different concepts related to money including saving, investing, and budgeting, and the consequences of their financial choices. These games promote critical thinking, strategic planning, and cooperation among the players. Through exposure to these games, players develop unique skill sets, a base that helps in their later life in making money-related decisions, thus, they are in line with being responsible and ensuring their success.

- ❖ **Weekly Pocket Money:** A lively game with the complex yet simple principles of money management, to provide a basis for the understanding of money, in an entertaining and enlightening manner. To play, your parents, grandparents, or any guardian will assist you by giving you some amount of pocket money at the beginning of the week. Then the little budget gets set up, and you are supposed to make the budget by dividing money into several categories including savings. During that period, you have to make a daily record of your expenses and savings, understanding, that you are required to sort out what you need and what you want while also considering the budget. When a child is actively involved in this activity, they develop important skills such as budgeting, saving, decision-making, and the understanding of the value of money. Furthermore, it has an aspect of responsibility and independence as they learn how to use money correctly within a given budget thus they are prepared to make tough decisions in the future. In a nutshell, Weekly Pocket Money Activity is a good way to make children aware of the cash management concepts that they will have to handle as they grow.

- ❖ **Saving Jars:** A super common activity that will help you understand how to keep records of money transactions and learn why you have to be attentive to how you spend your savings. You will be given jars or containers labelled with different tags like "spending," "saving" and "sharing." The money you want to spend for instance the money your parents gave you for doing chores perfectly or an allowance your parents gave. You will share how you divided up your earnings into the given jars, setting priorities on spending money. You can grasp the importance of managing their money, saving up, and considering their spending decisions to prevent overspending. It will help you understand major money skills including budgeting, prioritizing, and many more that build the base for good money-saving habits in the future.

- ❖ **Money Management Role-Play:** Another educational activity in which the teachers or group leaders put each student in different real-life scenarios with money as an important factor. This is one of the best ways to teach you money handling. You will be assigned a role based on different role-play scenarios. Each case outlines money-related topics, i.e. income, expenses, and future investments. Using scenarios that can be conducted via role-playing, you will justify your actions. After which you will receive the result of your actions' consequences in a safe environment. By doing this activity, students will learn how to solve problems while also developing communication skills and obtaining a good understanding of money management through this activity. The participants will get the necessary qualities for wisely managing their funds and confronting real-life financial issues that might spring up.

- ❖ **Second-Hand Products Hunt:** This activity can also be called "Thrift Store Hunt", which instructs the participants about the essence of saving, and spending carefully while contributing to safe and green earth as well. The main components in this activity are several thrift stores, flea markets, garage sales, or online selling platforms, including Facebook Marketplace or eBay. You have to find out where specific items are available at the best prices. Therefore, it's also about comparison shopping and bargaining ability. This lesson will help you to understand why comparison is necessary for saving the most, as well as how to highlight the highest spending tasks. Additionally, it is worth mentioning that everyone who purchases second-hand stuff will discover the reasons why you should be concerned about a greener earth. This operation, on the other side, supports effective communication and boosts fundamental skills including budgeting, and so on.

❖ **Online Games:** Among many other interactive and, mainly, entertaining online game apps that allow youngsters to learn about money management, there are those programmed specifically for this purpose. These games are either based on math or stories related to real life in which they do, for instance, the management of a company, investment, or spending within a budget. In many cases, these games use elements of decision-making, strategy, and risk management offering a valuable platform for learning money and related areas. You find out how your money and resource management matter, personalize the outcomes and improve critical thinking skills. Moreover, online gaming can be a team venture together with players, helping them cooperate as well as compete, teaching them to be great teammates and be responsible for their budgets. Online games enable players to put themselves into live money markets for a visual effect as well as being a source of entertainment and knowledge. Through this, you will learn money skills and be ready to face reality with an upper hand.

The integration of games and activities into daily life itself is still the most forward-looking way of encouraging my young comrades to learn money management skills. Individuals learn about budgeting, saving, spending, and investing through practical exercises such as the Weekly Pocket Money Activity, Saving Jars Activity, Money Management Role-Plays, Second-Hand Product Hunt, and Online Games. The activities allow the youth to experience real-life financial decisions and to understand the consequences of these decisions. They also allow them to learn from the successes and challenges of their own or others. By regularly practising and applying these knowledge skills in different scenarios, you will eventually get the confidence to manage money efficiently. These activities end up polishing youth by explaining valuable knowledge about thinking before making decisions and lifestyles that are key to creating a roadmap for success in the long term.

Strong leadership qualities include learning and handling a budget and saving money efficiently. Leaders with these skills can easily manage resources, achieve goals, build a trustworthy team, and boost their confidence. These skills will help you, as a leader to improve the growth of your company. In the same way, planning and spending your money, resources, and adaptability to changes will also help you sail through the harsh waters of the world. Therefore, leaders with such attributes can earn more trust and as a result, form better relations and thus enjoy strong support. Merging leadership and money management is the foundation for both good development of skills as a leader and business.

Chapter 16

Little Lamplighters

My fellow buddies, true leaders are not only strong, and confident, but also kind and compassionate and value each relationship in their lives. While strength and other qualities are important, they must maintain harmony with love, kindness, and compassion for everyone. A leader with all the leadership qualities earns the trust, respect, and loyalty of the community around him. This is not achieved by showing off power and wealth but by several acts of kindness, and care for others. Every healthy relationship we build is an important thread in the curtain of our leadership development, therefore it is our duty to value and support these relationships with gratitude and honesty. Let us attempt to be leaders who, in addition to motivating others to achieve greatness, also encourage and assist individuals in our surroundings, encouraging a community based on compassion, understanding, and respect for one another.

In this joyful trip, we will discover the mysteries of healthy relationships and understand the enchanted feelings of positive connections. Every chapter is a kind of a treasure hunt, where opening a new chapter brings to light a satisfying sound and every page carries a precious step in the journey of becoming a leader, like a hidden coin in your pocket. As you turn the pages you will discover that kindness is actually that special key that opens the door to close and healthy relationships between people. When we treat each other as though they are great people, we form a planet where all humans feel great and accepted.

As we all know it's not easy to form comfortable and healthy connections with others with effective communication only, which is why making the first moves and practicing conversation skills is necessary. If we look at the reason why kindness is a must in building strong bonds, we can see its importance in maintaining all sorts of relationships. The act of drawing attention to small actions means that being kind to others, despite little, can lead to many benefits for the whole society.

There's nothing that can beat the feeling of having positive and healthy connections with people. We will show the power of kindness together in building strong bonds. It could be a gesture of lending a hand, listening to someone, or saying a word of kindness. Whatever your way is, kindness in friendship will always benefit in terms of strengthening the social bond and will leave a mark on everyone's mind. My aspiring youth, look at the results of your caring actions, as they can warm everyone's hearts or even entire communities. The idea of compassion and generosity provides us with several opportunities to help create positive connections.

Just come and get into our bus, as we are about to rush to the next adventures of kindness and friendships. Shall we make a new start, learn, laugh, and grow together, as we unwrap the remaining treasures of positive and healthy connections and the happiness of making new friends? Let's GO, My Young Comrades!

Activities – Healthy Relationships

❖ **Magical Friendship Journey:** A creative and engaging function where you have an opportunity to discover the world of social life where you can make yourself as well as the other person happy. By taking part in this activity, you and your friends step into a fantasy world, and the different lands in them represent different characteristics of the bond of friendship. For example, they may pay a visit to the Land of Caring, the Land of Sympathy, the Land of Tolerance, as well as the Land of Speaking Out. In this adventurous journey, depending on the type of character, one faces different challenges, missions, and the adventure itself that promotes qualities like kindness, empathy, and communication skills. This activity teaches you valuable lessons about the need to treat others with love, be kind and respectful, communicate and listen, consider the needs of others, and communicate both ways honestly and openly. Through your social interaction with each other, you will pick up certain social and emotional skills, which are essential for building healthy relationships.

❖ **Treasure Hunt for Kindness:** This event has a purpose to teach the values of care, kindness, and sensitivity. Kindness can help develop positive and healthy relationships, which are set in the right direction. The game aims to separate the players into teams and provide them these challenges that are related to kindness. These challenges are made up of many actions like serving as a friend for a needy person, lending a helping hand, or committing an act of random kindness to a stranger. With every mission of completing a task, you will obtain a clue to the treasure's hidden location. While the activity organizers prepare to begin the hunt by sounding a horn, they make sure the teams engage in acts of compassion as the seekers find the goodies with support from fellow members as they find clues together. This activity surely will foster a lot of kindness among students, and it will help to discover teamwork, communication, and collaboration. Through actively being involved in the Treasure Hunt for Kindness, you will give value to the lesson of creating lasting and positive connections with your classmates through their acts of kindness as well as cooperation, which results in a more compassionate and open community.

- ❖ **Friendship Bingo:** Have you heard about bingo? Well, this is a unique type of bingo game as in this game the players can learn and improve their relationships with friends through establishing healthy and positive connections. To participate, all the players are given a bingo card that contains several friendship-building dares or acts, for example, "smile to a stranger", "invite someone to play games with you", "actively listen to a friend's story", and "tell a sweet compliment to someone". These acts should be finished and the respective squares on the cards should be marked. During these activities, you will work on social skills that are vital for becoming a compassionate leader namely, empathy, communication, and kindness. Not only does the "Friendship Bingo" game establish a culture of kindness that promotes a positive and compassionate environment but is also intended to promote an environment of belonging where everyone is accepted. By playing this game, you will get an idea of the importance of friendship building through giving small respectful favours and positive relationships.

- ❖ **Social Skills Role-Playing:** Interpersonal skills play an important role in success, that's why the game called "Social Skills Role-Playing" is effective and interactive for helping children develop essential social skills and build worthwhile and healthy relationships with other people. You along with the other participants are firstly divided into pairs or small groups and given scenarios to act, for example, the teacher might give you a scenario in which you will introduce yourself to a new friend, solve a conflict, or include someone who feels left out. But, through role-playing, you can improve your social skills that are valuable such as active listening, empathy, assertiveness, and problem solving. Through the method of becoming immersed in these social activities, children get experience and self-assurance in the real deal of conversations with classmates, which in turn, lead to more effective and positive social relations.

- ❖ **Kindness Corner:** A sweet activity with a warm hug to create an honest, caring, and compassionate environment where you and other children will share healthy and pleasant ways to relate with one another. It is an activity where everyone will take part in expressing or portraying acts of kindness they experienced or saw with their eyes. These could be gestures accompanying toy sharing, playing with a friend, or saying something good to others. Spend some time creating your own story or drawing, you can choose a good deed you already did or one you wish you could do. You can share your story and drawing with the group eventually, so your kind act will be an attractive story. As mentioned earlier, this occupation not only provides empathy and gratitude but also gives you a chance to pay respect and celebrate the kindness in your lives. The Kindness Corner, where children exchange their experiences, is a medium of learning the worth of positive, healthy, and caring links between friends and family through acts of kindness and sympathy. Finally, an improved social circle is built where your team members look up to you for support and encouragement.

- ❖ **Conversation Starters:** Developing social and effective communication skills through an interest-based activity that encourages children to make friends with and enjoy with other children is called the "Conversation Starters" activity. Everyone in the group is given conversation-starting opportunities, for example, "What's your favourite hobby?" or "Tell me about your pet." These questions will start the conversation and create an environment that will encourage fellow members to share their personal experiences and interests. As children apply conversation starters, they master skills of leading conversations and participating in the conversation with active listening and demonstrate a heart of interest in others. This engagement helps students develop empathy, communication, and comprehension at the same time. This creates a base that holds positive and healthy relationships among children. As a result of conversations and participation in activities, children start to notice the sense of being cared for and part of the group, which in many ways reflects authentic friendship bonds based on similar interests.

❖ **Friendship Bracelet Making:** An activity that promotes creative and healthy connections among friends while providing them with an environment where they can develop their artistic and creative side is the "Friendship Bracelet Making activity". You and your friends will get colored threads or beads, and make friendship bracelets that will fit perfectly for them. This would become a precious item that can be given or exchanged with each other to represent closeness and the fact that they are friends. This activity not only helps children in creative expression, but it also focuses on teamwork and cooperation as they give a hand to each other with the techniques and designs they suggest. During the process of making friendship bracelets, you will have an opportunity to hang out with your favourite thing and be involved in the same mission which helps them to build positive bonds. This activity sets the pace for these children to discover the value of sharing, empathy as well as respect for others, which is the first step in building healthy relationships.

❖ **Compliment Circle:** "The Compliment Circle" is a cheerful activity that encourages the formation of healthy and positive relationships through the establishment of a culture of kindness and appreciation. You and your classmates should gather around, sit in a circle and, one by one, offer each other compliments or words of gratitude in this activity. All the children may get appreciation and cheers from their comrades, which builds an encouraging and supportive atmosphere for all. This activity boosts self-confidence and esteem among the group members because the youngsters respect and praise each other for who they are and what their unique abilities and skills are. Through Compliment Circle, children learn that uplifting others and spreading positivity is the essence of welcoming and empathy which create a more supportive environment. This activity makes you and the other participants more compassionate, communicative, and kinder, thus providing a strong ground for building healthy relationships based on common respect and care.

❖ **Team-building Games:** "Team-building Games" are deeply engaging games that seek to develop cooperation, communication, and trust among children and, by this, create a healthy relationship between them. In the game, players are separated into groups and each team participates in different types of challenges or tasks that require cooperation and teamwork to be effective and successful. For example, one of them is building a tower with blocks, and another one is solving a puzzle or running an obstacle course. You will learn how to exchange ideas, how to listen to others, and how to care about each other. The team-building games help in developing empathy and understanding among children. At the end of team games, you will create a deep bond of team spirit and solidarity, which is the basis of your friendships built on respect and collaboration. This team-building activity offers collaboration, problem-solving, and skills to lay a foundation for building healthy and positive relationships within the group.

❖ **Story time:** An activity that creates an everlasting & wonderful experience; not only is it great fun but also helps to nourish positive relationships through the sharing of stories. In this activity, you and your friends will meet up to listen to stories that have themes such as friendship, empathy, and kindness. Then they are given the chance to write down the lessons that they learned from stories they have just heard and the reactions that they had. Through storytelling, everyone is pushed into the exciting realm of imagination, where they begin to feel sincere emotions with the characters, take different perspectives, and learn important life lessons. Through dialogue about the stories, the children get to practice expressing their feelings openly and freely. Thus, they can communicate openly and respectfully. Stories time brings people together and they create feelings of belonging and connection among them by sharing emotions and experiences. The purpose of this exercise is to bring empathy, communication, and connectivity, essential elements of creating healthy and positive relationships.

❖ To sum up, the activities that promote leadership qualities such as kindness, empathy, and positive and healthy connections, improve social skills and help us move forward on the path to becoming a compassionate leader. You can hone your leadership skills by activity taking part in these activities. Building strong bonds and fostering deep connections helps us grow into compassionate leaders who lead with honesty, understanding, and a sincere desire to uplift and inspire others. Through our dedication to building strong relationships and developing empathy, we encourage everyone around us to follow suit, spreading kindness and good deeds around the world.

No matter, if the benefits of becoming a future leader might be eye-catching, it is the long journey that really counts. Whether it is the friendship bingo or kindness circles, doing all these activities will generate joy, and pride, and ensure that the experience remains a great and unforgettable memory.

Chapter 17

Courage Captains

Most of you are strong enough to bounce back after a hard time. Do you know this is a well-known quality and its name is resilience? For those who are hearing this word for the first time, resilience is the ability to bounce back or recover from setbacks or difficult times. This quality develops when you experience different challenges in life and deal with them positively. For example, when something negative is going on in your life, you feel different emotions based on the event, such as pain, sorrow, and anger, but you manage to push through and move forward physically and mentally.

My young companions, we shall embark on an adventurous journey of learning resilience together with the help of ups and downs in life. Just like how Tarzan moves through the jungle to areas where he hasn't seen before and fights through the challenges he faces, resilience helps you take on challenges head-on with determination. The main part is when things become harder, learn from the mishaps, and come back stronger with each experience. Each hardship will develop you into a more resilient and stronger person. So, gear up, believe in yourself, be up for the challenge, and smash your way forward through the challenges!

Just like plants need sunlight and water as a requirement for their growth, life challenges need your courage and determination to turn into exciting chances for growth. There is no bigger excitement than when you need to overcome a challenge and you see the path, of how you did it, shining behind. Every time you conquer a challenge, this becomes a chance for you to develop new skills, become stronger, and see what sort of hero you really are. My little leaders, instead of feeling scared, anxious, or sad when facing a challenge, remember that it's a real adventure with a whole universe full of ups and downs.

Do you know with resilience there comes perseverance? Perseverance is a unique type of superpower that will push you to keep on going forward. Suppose you are climbing a tall mountain, and as you know it can be very difficult. After some time, you are tired and want to stop there. Perseverance is like a backpack full of extra, hidden energy, which allows you to keep going even when things get tough. It's giving in, even if you can't write another letter. When you do not give up, you demonstrate your power to the world and the lengths you can go to. It doesn't matter if it is riding a bicycle, preparing for an exam, or even developing a new friendship, perseverance – your good friend – will be your companion throughout the journey. In a nutshell, perseverance is the key, the highest mountain, the most difficult task, they do not exist for you! You will get where your mind is!

Hey kiddos, as we can see our journey has many ups and downs just like a bumpy road. As you walk on this path, you will most likely encounter different types of obstacles, big or small. Remember you have a superpower inside you that will help you force through the challenges. Imagine yourself as a knight in shining armour with a mission, you will encounter dragons and difficult mazes on the way. And with perseverance as your faithful companion, you'll be able to cut down the obstacles and meet the goals.

From mastering new skills, making new friends, or even dealing with difficult homework, you need to keep on pushing and keep your eyes on the prize. Every single challenge becomes a stepping-stone to your goal of success, and with true spirit, you can overcome all of them! Moreover, each difficulty presents you with some new lessons. For example, you can know how strong you can be if you persevere, how creative you can be when you are thinking about the solution, and how much you can take when you face setbacks. So, be courageous enough to face your challenges as they will help you discover your special powers and improve daily! In the end, you gain wisdom, strength, and courage to approach life's greater adventures!

If you think you are not strong or courageous enough to bounce back from difficulties, take a deep breath as it's completely okay. Not everyone is courageous or resilient from childhood, sometimes you need someone to help you in lighting the fire and spirit inside of you. So let's make yourself shine by actively taking part in the activities of building resilience. Once you are done, ask yourself, do you feel stronger?

Activities – Building Resilience

❖ **Trust Walk:** The Trust Walk is an inviting activity that helps to raise resilience in a group and to promote trust. Pair off the students, with one being blindfolded, and the other one being the guiding one. The guide is taking their blindfolded partner through a walking course in which the only source of information is the verbal commands and physical help that you offer to pass obstacles and challenges. With this exercise, barriers between class members are removed, and trust between them is also built. The blindfolded have to trust and rely on the guide whom they see as extra support and also adapt to unknown and sudden situations. When you start loosening the grip on control and let your partners do their part in the tasks, you are building up the required strength of character such as stepping over the hurdles in the way of resilience. In addition to that, Trust Walk develops empathy as both partners face vulnerability and dependence, which leads to deeper friendship and greater unity as a team.

❖ **Musical Chairs:** Musical chairs is a super famous and one of the most common games out there, and they can be used to develop resilience. Almost everyone is very much aware of the game where chairs are arranged in a group like a circle with one less chair than the number of participants. When the music is playing, children may walk or dance around the chairs, and when the music stops, everyone then should sit down in any of the available chairs. The person left out without a chair is eliminated, and one seat is taken out in the next round. This is what continues until only one person is left. In this game, resilience is taught by involving children in a changing environment and then competing with them when their luck runs. If we consider losing and other factors of this game, players will develop being focused and able to make quick decisions and overcome the feeling of disappointment. Additionally, the game becomes more challenging, and as chairs are eliminated, participants have to draw on their hidden strengths to win in the end.

❖ **Hula-Hoop Team Challenge:** Unlike the simple hula-hoop, this team challenge is a lot more difficult. The Hula-Hoop Team Challenge is usually organized in schools to create an environment where the students can develop teamwork and resilience in an engaging yet memorable way. The teacher will split the kids into groups and give the entire group a hula hoop. The task they have to pay attention to is the passing of the hula hoop around the team without letting it touch the ground or break into the chain. In playing this game, the students learn resilience through effectively communicating, team collaborating, and adapting to changing conditions. As the hula hoop moves around the circle, teams can meet with obstacles or moments of unbalance that test their skills to stay focused and cooperative so that the hoop's momentum doesn't stop. Team members become better at trusting each other, helping each other out, encouraging one another, and being resilient. Beyond this, it also boosts creativity, and critical thinking, making you more resilient through teamwork, communication, and adaptability.

❖ **Resilience Bingo:** A game that is a playful and educational tool to help young people develop a good supportive system and be resilient. Each participant will get a bingo card with different resilience-based challenges written into the squares such as "Do something new " or "Practice gratitude... Try to face a fear." Once you complete the task, you have to mark these squares like a simple bingo game. This game motivates you and your friends to go beyond their comfort zones, face their fears, and develop healthy ways to tackle life's challenges. Through active participation in resilience-focused activities, the participants create their development plans to improve their learning, strengthen their skills, and develop the spirit of achievement when they face challenges. Resilience Bingo nurtures strong community ties and support as players share their game experiences and cheer one another on all through the game, hence promoting resilience through personal awareness, and positive acts.

❖ **Obstacle Course Challenge:** An activity that is both energizing and testing and also helps build resilience by helping children overcome obstacles and hardships. The competitors run through a sequence of physical drills including climbing over walls, crawling under ropes, hopping over fences, or balancing on beams. Every obstacle symbolizes a literal jump in life, and you need to be mentally prepared and persevere to the end. This hike pushes resilience through participants facing their fears of rough terrain, adapting to a mixed environment, and overcoming their negative emotions. You will acquire resilience as you endure both failures and successes with a positive attitude, problem-solving, and continued focus even when faced with tough challenges.

❖ **The Resilience Tower:** A team task that aims at enhancing resilience skills and developing personal growth. The participants are given some building materials such as blocks, or Legos and their task is to build their strong tower together. There is a twist in this activity – the tower should stand not only against specific threats, like strong winds, simulated earthquakes, or extra weight, but it should also stay in the upright position. This activity creates resilience, due to the need for the participants to cooperate, change the way they act, and persevere if they come across any difficulty. Confronted with problems the tower faces, the participants try to solve the problems, communicate effectively, and follow a flexible approach. Students who face setbacks during the building process develop resilience by defeating opponents through perseverance, teamwork, and innovative problem-solving.

❖ **Emotion Charades:** An extremely lively and interactive game where the participants have the chance to explore and express a wide variety of emotions, take courage from each other, and build resiliency. The acting will start after player A acts emotion out without speaking and player B or the rest of the team guesses the emotion that was demonstrated. In turn, each student is assigned a role representing a unique feeling. This activity is useful as it brings about resilience by teaching people emotional awareness. Children develop the ability to distinguish and name different types of emotions, both positive and negative. Moreover, by acting and observing the emotions of others, the members can develop empathy and understanding towards different emotional experiences. This is an important element that enhances resilience because it builds supportive relationships and effective communication. Furthermore, this activity offers a secure place for the participants to reveal themselves and practice vulnerability, which are the key factors of resilience since they generate the desire to seek advice and cope with hardship more effectively. In this lighthearted but powerful exercise, the participants not only hone their emotional resilience but also fortify their social skills and a sense of belonging to the group.

❖ **Puzzle Relay Race:** An action-packed race where you and your friends should work together, solve problems, and be adaptable to make them resilient. The pieces of a puzzle are given to each team to find a solution. Nevertheless, instead of competing to solve the puzzle separately, the group members have to be in sync and coordinate to complete the puzzle as fast as possible. The catch is that everybody on the team can only spend a certain amount of time working on the puzzle before passing it on to the person in front of them. By asking students to consistently show off their communication skills, effectively manage their time, and maintain attention, this exercise helps participants develop resilience. Teams that encounter difficulties have to change course fast and keep going until they reach the race's finish line. Building resilience requires children to accept that life is unpredictable, adapt to changing scenarios, and depend on and support one another.

❖ **Mindfulness Moments:** A soothing and mindful practice that develops resiliency skills by helping individuals build self-awareness, emotional regulation, and stress management techniques. Children who take part in the activity meet in a friendly environment and practice mindfulness through guided mindfulness exercises, for example, deep breathing. The activity focuses on concentrating on the present, feeling and registering every thought and sensation without any judgment, and creating an atmosphere of calm and serenity within. This way, it contributes to the creation of a more resilient person to enable them to deal with the stress, anxiety, and other challenges that may come up in life. Training mindful practice teaches children to witness their emotions and thoughts without being crippled by them, hence allowing them to manage difficult scenarios with focus and calmness. Mindfulness Moments also teaches self-compassion and acceptance, the core aspects of resilience that allow a person to treat oneself in a kind and loving manner.

❖ **Resilience Board Game:** This board game is an entertaining and learner-friendly game that can help you master resilience skills through engaging gameplay. The players will move to different spots through the roll of the dice or using cards drawn. These scenarios will test their resilience. Whether it is confronting failures, emotional management, situational skills, or stress-buster practices, these situations are learning opportunities. To progress, players must utilize resilience strategies such as problem-solving, positive thinking, looking for support, and practising self-reflection. This skill is developed through the exploration of several challenges and well-thought-out decisions and includes; adaptability, and perseverance. The game also, promotes discussion and sharing experiences, therefore, nurturing an environment that enhances social support where they develop each other and become resilient together. The game of Resilience is designed to provide learning through interactive gameplay to equip the players with skills needed to form a resilient character that can be applied to real-life situations.

- ❖ **Goal-Setting Collage:** One of the creative and empowering activities that help individuals to become resilient is visualizing their aspirations and developing realistic and achievable goals. First, you gather newspapers, art supplies, and many others, as well as poster boards or big sheets of paper. Next, each participant will reflect on their personal goals, aspirations, and the areas they want to improve in, like academics, career, personality, health, or some other goals. With the help of art and stationery supplies, you can form collages that visually represent your goals and dreams, while blending with images, words, and phrases. This activity nurtures resilience through the act of holding a clear purpose, necessary motivation, and power in the ability to express goals and visualize desired outcomes. Children also reflect on themselves while creating their collages, by identifying the problems they may have and suggesting solutions to the problems, thus, building resilience capability. They can share their collages with others and this can give them support which can take the form of feedback, encouragement, and accountability, as this will help them become stronger as they work harder to achieve their goals.

- ❖ **Stress Ball Art:** The Stress Ball Art is a therapeutic activity that helps children in dealing with stress and express emotions through art. During the process of this activity, students collect stress balls and art supplies including markers, paints, or other art materials. Next, each participant fetches their stress ball and then decorates it according to their style using the art stuff. The use of artistic techniques in this activity develops individual resilience by involving participants in self-expression and creativity - the two elements crucial for self-management and stress relief. During the process of decorating stress balls, children get the chance to look within themselves, name their feelings, and redirect any negativity into positive and constructive alternatives.

- ❖ **Resilience Journal:** This activity tends to make our resilience stronger through self-awareness, gratitude, and individual growth. If you have a journal or a notebook, where you can constantly register your thoughts, emotions, and experiences related to resilience, it is more than enough. Participants should set a time each day or week to engage with their journal of resilience, reviewing the moments when they were strong, felt growing, and also overcame the challenges. Moreover, you can use the journal to write thankful letters, set goals, and observe the progress you are making toward being resilient in your life. It's a great way of building resilience since it teaches a positive mindset, self-reflection, and coping practices when dealing with obstacles. Through journaling, people can identify growth opportunities and recognize their resilient strengths. This aids in the person's development of resilience qualities including flexibility and determination as well as building on their strengths. The Resilience Journal is an incredible tool for self-examination and personal growth that can help you become more resilient to challenges in life.

A sense of resilience is a good thing no matter which age you are at but as you get old, resilience too develops with growing age. In the same manner, as a little seed can be turned into a big, strong tree of its own, your resilience will grow with you when you face the various challenges of life. At early ages, you start to grow resilience by learning to get back on your feet after little bumps, like a scratched knee or a lost toy. Being older means you will face more problems such as challenging school tasks or quarrels with mates. Such experiences bring you to the stage where you develop more resilience by teaching you to be able to adjust, solve problems, and keep going forward even when obstacles show up. Therefore, just keep in mind that each difficulty you get through builds up a new layer of your resilience and your life goes on. You get stronger and can handle any unexpected challenge!

Don't ever stop appreciating your parents as they are the ones who introduced you to resilience! Just like how the superhero's sidekick is there to lend a hand and words of wisdom to us when we face difficulties, parents are always there to provide support. They are our source of motivation, shouting encouragement from within as we tumble through the hills and valleys of life. Whether it's taking on boring homework, dealing with bullies, or hugging us in times of utmost need, parents take the major responsibility of building our resilience. They teach us the skills we will use in life, like problem-solving and continuing to try, and they show us that it's okay to make mistakes, because those are part of learning and growing. In case you face a difficulty, bear in mind that your parents are there for you to help you as you evolve to be the strong, awesome individual that you are designed to be! They will help you achieve your dream of becoming a future leader and will be proud of you.

Chapter **18**

Tech Titans

You love playing games on the mobile phone, or drawing art on a tablet, don't you? My young children, we all are familiar with the fact that technology plays a vital role in our lives. As time goes on, the use of technology becomes more widespread. I can't deny that excessive use of technology tends to cause harm to you guys, but if you use technology within a certain limit, it will positively affect your development.

Wondering how?

There are several advantages to technology-based activities for kids' development. The primary benefit that comes from technology is getting new learning opportunities for you. You can easily access the world full of information at your fingertips with the help of the internet. Not only that, you can find answers to your questions with a few clicks and learn topics at their own pace. Along with parental guidance, technology can provide my enthusiastic future leaders with a safe environment to explore.

Using technology, you can easily be in touch with others; your friends, family or relatives that are living far away from you. Improved communication skills will help you develop important social skills, for example, empathy, and cooperation. You will become more confident and express yourself better.

Remember, digital art and music is an important method of expressing your creative side. This will help you develop a stronger sense of identity, and boost your confidence and self-esteem. Not only that, technology can help you learn how to solve difficult problems in creative ways as it makes you think outside the box.

When you do tasks that call for precise movements, such as using a computer mouse or touchscreen, your coordination and motor abilities improve. Playing video games requires fast reflexes and good hand-eye coordination, which helps to improve these abilities. Furthermore, research indicates that specific forms of technology might enhance memory and focus. For example, youngsters who engage in action video games have been found to have higher working memory, while educational apps have been linked to greater memory recall.

Additionally, technology makes it easier to learn about a variety of cultures, giving them the chance to interact with individuals from all over the world and gain knowledge of different customs and beliefs. If you embrace technology, you are better prepared for a world where digital literacy will be increasingly important, enabling them to take advantage of possibilities and successfully navigate a changing environment. Technology may be an effective tool for developing critical skills that promote all-round development when used responsibly and under parental supervision. This will help in ensuring that you guys are ready for the opportunities and challenges that lie ahead.

Unfortunately, even if I acknowledge and promote the benefits of technology in children's lives, it is equally important to consider the flaws and possible risks linked with its excessive use. The possibility of addiction and usage is the most important of these worries. Overexposure to screens can cause sleep patterns to be disturbed and physical activity levels to drop, which can lead to a poor lifestyle and some health problems. Additionally, extended screen time can cause anxiety, reduced self-esteem, promote isolation and lack of motivation, which are harmful to kids' mental health.

The possibility of being exposed to inappropriate content through technological means is another urgent concern. Even with efforts to make internet spaces kid-friendly, you may still come across offensive or violent content that could be harmful to their mental and emotional development. Furthermore, these concerns are made worse by cyberbullying and online harassment, which severely damages children's emotional well-being and weakens their confidence and self-worth.

Technology has an effect on youngsters' physical and mental health that goes beyond just exposing them to negative content. Increased screen usage has been associated in studies with higher levels of anxiety and sadness as well as focus and concentration problems. Additionally, the widespread impact of social media networks can uphold unattainable ideals of success and attractiveness, which can give rise to feelings of incompetence and low self-esteem. To address these issues, a comprehensive strategy that strikes a balance between the advantages of technology and preemptive steps to reduce any possible harm to your general well-being is needed.

Activities – Learn with Technology

❖ **Digital Scavenger Hunt:** One of the most innovative activities that develops necessary leadership qualities among the players with the help of technology. In this activity, members are entrusted with finding and capturing clues or objects utilizing smartphones, tablets, or cameras. Through collaboration, communication, and vital consideration, members must work together to disentangle clues, unravel puzzles, and explore different challenges. You need a bunch of people to play this game and enjoy it to the fullest. Ask everyone to list dares and riddles, and when everyone is connected to the online conference, give each member a chance to tell their dare or riddle. At that time, the rest of the participants will give their best to fulfil that dare. This movement polishes leadership qualities such as cooperation, problem-solving, and decision-making. Pioneers rise as people who take charge, facilitate endeavours, and motivate their group individuals to drive forward and adjust to changing circumstances. Moreover, members learn to use technology appropriately and show creativity, all of which are crucial abilities for being a true leader from the beginning. Overall, the activity "Digital Scavenger Hunt" gives an energetic and interactive stage for developing and polishing leadership qualities while using modern technology to grasp the opportunities.

❖ **Follow Along:** An engaging activity which can help in teaching leadership qualities through active participation, dynamic support and collaboration. In "Follow Along", you will be paired into small groups with the other participants, with an individual assigned as the captain and the other as the team members. The leader is entrusted with directing their accomplice through an arrangement of challenges, which may include problem-solving, physical hardships, or creativity. Through effective communication, compassion, and successful guidance, you will learn to motivate and encourage your team members to overcome hardships and accomplish shared objectives. In the meantime, players obtain fundamental qualities such as active listening, versatility, and team collaboration as they follow the leader's course. By substituting parts, members pick up a better understanding of leadership and the significance of mutual respect and participation in accomplishing victory. Eventually, "Follow Along" cultivates the advancement of leadership qualities such as communication, compassion, versatility, and collaboration, planning members to lead viably in different individual, academic, and professional settings.

❖ **Online Cooperative Games:** Online coop games offer a captivating stage for instilling leadership qualities through collaborative gameplay and key decision-making. In these recreation games, players work together towards common targets, requiring clear and effective communication, on-point cooperation, and problem-solving skills. Leaders rise as people take on parts that include coordinating with the group, understanding the objectives, and giving direction to attain the shared goals. By exploring challenges together, players learn to use each other's qualities, adjust to changing circumstances, and make collective choices that advantage the group. Through gameplay, members create qualities such as communication, compassion, and flexibility, as they learn to lead by case, develop trust, and cultivate a supportive group environment. Eventually, online coop games give an enjoyable stage for developing leadership skills that are basic for victory in both virtual and real-world scenarios.

❖ **Web Quest:** An informative activity that not only promotes learning but also improves team collaboration, and critical thinking skills. In this quest, members are entrusted with investigating online and finding information to assemble data and solve a particular issue or challenge. As participants explore through different websites, analyze data, and write down discoveries, they develop essential skills such as problem-solving, and decision-making. Additionally, members frequently work in groups, which requires effective communication, cooperation, and distribution of tasks. Through the method of planning, organizing, and executing on the Web Quest, members obtain leadership qualities such as communication, organization, and versatility, as they learn to collaborate successfully, propel their peers, and navigate complex assignments. Eventually, this activity gives an energetic and intelligent stage for developing leadership skills.

❖ **Virtual Bingo:** An exact copy of the traditional bingo game except that it is digital, which means it is played on different devices such as phones, laptops, and PCs. There is no difference in the rules, you have to complete a specific type of line either diagonal or straight. If you want to play a virtual bingo, you have to select a card or generate a random card. Each card has around 25 words in a 5 by 5 section. Once your friends join and are ready or any stranger is ready, you can set an automatic draw of the next bingo word. In such a manner, on equal time intervals, a word is revealed and whenever a word shows up, you have to mark it on the virtual card if it is a match. As soon as the pattern is complete, participants can claim their bingos, the one who gets it first wins. "Virtual Bingo" isn't only an amusement but a stage for enhancing unique qualities through engagement, communication, and collaboration. Members are encouraged to connect, promoting social connection and communication qualities. You will learn how to organize the game, effectively communicate, and keep up eagerness among players. As game leaders guide through the game, it illustrates their qualities such as active participation, communication, and sympathy. Also, Virtual Bingo promotes collaboration and participation as members work together to attain a common objective – winning the diversion. Through this collaborative approach, members develop leadership as they explore challenges and celebrate victories together. Eventually, Virtual Bingo gives a fun and intuitive platform for developing administration abilities that are essential for success.

❖ **Office Trivia:** Office Trivia serves as a special road for developing leadership qualities inside a professional environment. This activity pushes members to a friendly competition while testing their information on office-related tasks and trivia. Everyone gets a chance to organize the trivia, ask questions, and facilitate the event. Besides, "Office Trivia" cultivates teamwork and collaboration as members work together to reply to questions and strategize their approach. Leaders illustrate compelling communication skills by guaranteeing everybody has a chance to contribute and cultivating a comprehensive environment. Furthermore, the amusement promotes adaptability and strength as members explore through challenges and unforeseen turns within the trivia questions. Overall, this activity gives a unique stage for developing and polishing leadership abilities such as communication, cooperation, flexibility, and adaptability.

❖ **Virtual Volunteering:** "Virtual Volunteering" offers a one-of-a-kind opportunity to develop leadership qualities through online engagement and community interaction. In this virtual activity, members have the chance to engage in leadership roles by organizing and planning virtual volunteering activities. You have to step up to organize virtual meetings, distribute tasks, and motivate volunteers to contribute their time and skills properly. Through virtual stages, you will illustrate communication, organization, and problem-solving qualities as you facilitate with group individuals, give them direction, and ensure the effective use of volunteer exercises. Furthermore, "Virtual Volunteering" cultivates compassion and sympathy as you will link with community members and create a positive effect on society. By driving virtual volunteer programs, members create necessary leadership qualities such as communication, teamwork, empathy, versatility, and activity, making them lead with passion.

❖ **Egg Drop:** A practical yet virtual activity that not only challenges your mind's activeness but also cultivates leadership skills through cooperation and problem-solving. In this action, members are entrusted with planning and building a structure that can ensure a raw egg is not cracked or broken when dropped from a certain height. Participants gather materials such as straws, paper cups, tape, rubber bands, and cotton balls, and then work individually or in teams to construct their egg protection devices. Once the structures are built, they are dropped from the predetermined height, and participants observe whether the egg inside remains intact or breaks. After each drop, participants reflect on their designs, make modifications, and repeat the dropping process as desired. The winner can be determined based on criteria such as whose egg survived the most drops or whose design was the most effective overall. Furthermore, "Egg Drop" empowers creativity as participants explore different materials and plans to realize the required result. You will illustrate versatility as you explore difficulties and alter your approach to guarantee victory to the extent.

❖ **Virtual Office Board Games:** An interesting collection of board games which play a vital role in developing leadership qualities through smooth collaboration and critical thinking. In these digital variations of classic board games, members have an opportunity to obtain true leadership skills by guiding their teams through different challenges and tasks. To play the board games, participants gather in a virtual space equipped with online board game platforms or applications. Each participant joins the game remotely using their computer or mobile device. The chosen game is then initiated, and participants take turns interacting with the game board and other players through the virtual interface. Through active listening, effective communication and decision-making, participants direct their group in defining terms, adjusting to changing elements, and accomplishing common objectives. Additionally, "Virtual Office Board Diversions" cultivate cooperation and comradeship as members work together to overcome obstacles and defeat opponents. Leaders illustrate versatility and resilience as they explore vulnerabilities and mishaps inside the game, rousing their group to persevere towards triumph. Virtual Office Board Games provide a platform for developing leadership qualities such as communication, teamwork, strategic thinking, adaptability, and resilience, all within a digital context.

Everyone loves playing games on their PC or laptop, who doesn't? These are the best activities in the entire book, as it involves many online games on your favorite device, either phone or laptop. I strongly believe you all will enjoy the most doing these activities.

As you know by now, technology has its unique set of advantages and drawbacks, we should limit the use of technology in such a way that it benefits us only. It can be one of the best and most engaging ways of developing leadership skills. Eventually, the digital world demonstrates a breathtaking adventure-ready with openings for positive leadership and individual development. Using technology as a source of motivation and development can encourage children to saddle their potential for useful purposes. It is necessary to define appropriate technology use and behaviour, growing mindful and careful users of these devices, who understand the significance of judgment in online interactions. Despite potential dangers, we must emphasize the positive perspectives of technology, encouraging curiosity and exploration while preparing children with the skills to explore online spaces safely.

Technology's part in today's life is indisputable, as it offers vast learning opportunities that rise above conventional boundaries. By grasping knowledge and experiences, children can develop basic leadership skills, imagination, and collaboration, preparing them to flourish in an ever-evolving world. Inevitably, by cultivating a culture of mindfulness and morals, we empower children to be compassionate leaders who use innovation for the more prominent good, driving positive change in their communities.

Chapter **19**
Leadership Marvels

Remember my fellow comrades, celebrating your leadership journey is fundamental for fostering a positive environment and recognizing your minor and major achievements. By recognizing these journeys, you can motivate others and inspire them to be strong leaders too. These journeys regularly include overcoming hardships, dealing with risks, and making noteworthy commitments to achieve your goal. Hence, it's critical to celebrate these turning points and achievements.

Welcoming leadership ventures allows highlighting the different ways people took to be compelling and true leaders. Whether it's through formal leadership programs, mentorship, or individual encounters, each moment is interesting and deserves to be celebrated. Sharing these stories can motivate you to seek after your leader's vision and contribute to your success in life.

When you celebrate the achievements in your leadership journey, it also strengthens the esteem of continuous learning. By reflecting on past encounters, leaders can distinguish zones for change and create ways for future victory. This way of handling self-reflection and learning is important for your growth.

Besides, it also cultivates a sense of community and comradeship inside groups. When people feel esteemed and acknowledged for their commitments, they are more likely to be encouraged to perform at their best. Recognizing leadership journeys can reinforce bonds among group members and create a collaborative environment where everybody feels engaged to succeed.

You know what's truly cool? The reality is that you're on a path to becoming the future little leader! Correct, that's right, you're like a superhero in preparing and gearing up for astonishing adventures ahead.

To begin with, being a leader means you get to create a real difference within the world around you. Whether at school, in the play area, or your community, you get the superpower to motivate others, offer assistance to your companions, and make things easier for everybody.

But that's not all! Your leadership journey is aiming to be stuffed with all sorts of great experiences. You'll try new things, learn from your poor mistakes, and find how awesome you truly are and can be. Each challenge you confront and each difficulty you overcome will make you stronger.

Being a leader isn't telling others what to do. It's way more than that, it's about being a great listener, an extraordinary partner, and a caring companion. You'll learn about team cooperation, effective communication, and empathy—skills that will assist you not only as it were as a pioneer but also in each perspective of your life.

But here's the finest part: this journey is all about YOU and YOU only! It includes finding what makes you one of a kind, what makes you energetic and full of passion, and what kind of leader you want to be. So, be prepared to unleash your hidden superhero, because the world is waiting for you to step up and make it a better place for everyone.

So, are you excited!? Since I SURELY am! Your leadership path will be one epic experience, filled with fun, learning, and tons of astonishing surprises. So, buckle up and get prepared to make an appearance for the world and show how magnificent you can be!

It's a useful exercise to reflect on your leadership development as it gives you awareness of your areas of strength, weakness, and improvement. You may evaluate your leadership development and identify the talents you've acquired by reflecting on your past experiences. You may recognize growth opportunities and recognize how far you've gone by reflecting on the difficulties you've encountered as well as your accomplishments.

Self-reflection is the process of identifying your strengths and traits as a leader. Spend some time reflecting on the traits and skills that help you succeed in your position. Maybe you're good at encouraging others, fixing problems, or communicating. Acknowledging your abilities helps you lead more successfully by enabling you to use them and boosting your confidence.

In the exact same way, taking account of your flaws lets you see where you can improve. Perhaps you have trouble deciding what to do, managing your time, or handling conflicts. Acknowledging your shortcomings will allow you to take early steps to improve them, such as getting more training, looking for a mentor, or exercising new abilities.

For personal development, thinking back on the difficulties you've faced as a leader is also essential. Think about the challenges you've encountered and the ways you overcame them. You may grow resilient, learn from setbacks, and modify your strategy going forward by thinking back on previous events. Every obstacle is a chance for growth and learning, so don't be afraid to take stock of your difficult moments.

Continuing your leadership learning journey in the right direction may be achieved by setting targets based on your ideas. Think about your goals as a leader and the areas you wish to concentrate on. Setting specific objectives provides you with a path to success plan and keeps you driven to go forward, whether you aim to take on more duties, strengthen your bonds with your team, or improve your communication skills.

Getting input from other people is another important part of evaluation. Seek feedback on your leadership style, areas of strength, and areas for progress from your peers, mentors, or superiors. Positive criticism offers insightful viewpoints and insights that can help you better grasp your leadership strengths and areas for improvement.

Personal growth requires fostering self-awareness and the acceptance of accomplishments. One helpful strategy is to engage in regular reflection activities. People who make time in their schedules for self-examination might keep journals in which they record their experiences, assets, and opportunities for growth. Through the development of mindfulness and gaining insights into one's thoughts, feelings, and actions, this practice helps people become more self-aware.

To further enhance self-awareness, a system of feedback must be created in addition to self-reflection. Growth is facilitated by creating an environment of open communication where people feel at ease asking for and accepting helpful criticism. People may better understand their areas of strength and progress when they get honest feedback, which provides insightful information about areas that require work and areas of strength.

Through the establishment of SMART goals—Specific, Measurable, Achievable, Relevant, and Time-bound—people may make a connection to their goals and monitor their leadership development over time. Celebrating little victories and accomplishments along the road helps people recognize their progress and promotes healthy and positive behaviour.

To begin, discovering new things is like embarking on a thrilling journey every day! It's also a ton of fun and maintains our curiosity and activity levels! There's always something new to learn, whether it's about baking cookies, dinosaurs, or space exploration. But learning new things never stops being enjoyable; it makes us develop into better versions of ourselves. Gaining confidence and independence is a result of learning new skills, such as tying our shoes or riding a bike. Additionally, learning about various individuals, groups, and ideologies broadens our perspective and increases our awareness of the world.

Continuous learning continues to help in resolving problems You know those moments of difficulty, such as when we're trying to figure out a challenging problem or learn a new game? We do, however, improve slightly each time we attempt again and learn from our errors. Like when you advance in a computer game, every obstacle you overcome makes you more robust.

Additionally, gaining new knowledge offers up a world of opportunities for the future. Who knows where it may lead us if we find a passion for music, science, or the arts one day? We have more opportunities to explore and follow our aspirations the more knowledge we have. Therefore, my buddy, never give up on growing and learning! Every small piece of knowledge, whether from reading books, asking questions, or trying something new, gets us one step closer to being the amazing, powerful superheroes we were destined to be!

Let's now discuss something really exciting: exploration and curiosity! Like Indiana Jones or Dora the Explorer, see yourself as an adventurer who is discovering the incredible universe full of knowledge that surrounds you! You see, having a curious mentality entails a constant desire to learn more, wondering how systems function, and posing questions. It's similar to possessing a superpower that enables you to learn tons of interesting facts about the universe.

Thus, what can we do to foster this wonderful spirit of inquiry and discovery? To start with, don't ever stop asking questions! There's never a dumb question, whether it's about how birds fly or why the sky is blue. Putting forward questions is like unlocking doors leading to new realms of knowledge and wisdom.

Now let us begin seeking information about everything surrounding us! Go for a stroll outside and observe your surroundings. Take note of the hues of the flowers, the patterns of the clouds, and the bird noises. If we listen closely enough, every small object has a tale to tell. Remember to try new things as well! Every new experience offers the chance to learn and grow, whether it's tasting a new dish, picking up a new pastime, or reading a new book. Who knows? You may uncover a new interest or overlooked skill!

The most crucial thing to remember is to have fun with it! Curiosity and exploration should never be forced upon us. It's about enjoying the process of learning, whether you're doing a science experiment, cracking a puzzle, or just wondering about the secrets of the cosmos. So, my friends, let's embrace our inner adventurers and set off on a fantastical quest of inquiry and discovery together!

Making a significant, long-lasting influence that goes beyond one's tenure in a leadership position is at the centre of the notion of leaving a positive leadership legacy. The goal is to leave a legacy that improves, empowers, and inspires people's lives today and in the future. A leader who wants to have a good impact prioritizes forming strong bonds with others, encouraging a climate of trust and cooperation, and training future generations of leaders. They leave a legacy of growth and empowerment by fostering a friendly atmosphere where people feel appreciated, respected, and inspired to realize their greatest potential.

Furthermore, a leader who is dedicated to building a positive legacy places a high value on moral leadership and social responsibility. They make moral judgments by taking into account how actions may affect individuals, communities, and the environment in the long run. Through their advocacy of justice, equity, and inclusion, they create a lasting legacy of constructive social change. Also, a true leader maintains a positive legacy and commits to creativity and constant progress. They promote exploration, learning, and creativity, developing a bright culture that pushes their team's growth and flexibility in response to changing circumstances. They leave behind a legacy of advancement and resiliency by welcoming change and fresh ideas.

My young companions, take some time out and do the following:

❖ Think about the things that bring you joy or excitement. It could involve looking out for other people, safeguarding animals, or maintaining the environment.

❖ Think about the role models in your life, such as scientists or superheroes. How much of an influence do they have, and how you can do something like that?

❖ Soak in your surroundings. Do you have any suggestions for improvements or changes to what you see? Perhaps it's assisting a stranger in need or tidying up a park.

❖ Consider the impression you wish to leave on others. Do you want to be renowned for your bravery, compassion, or inventiveness? Consider the traits you find admirable and how you may demonstrate them via your behaviour.

❖ Begin with little steps and then take action. You don't need to alter the world overnight! Every small deed, whether it's lending a hand to a buddy, clearing up garbage, or sharing toys, counts.

❖ Never forget that errors are normal throughout the journey. Growing and learning are components of the process. Thus, don't be scared to take risks and explore where your influence might lead you!

❖ No matter how big or little, you may start to make a difference by considering the influence you want to have on the world. So go ahead and have big dreams because you can make a positive difference in the world! In the end, leadership is about making a difference by leaving a legacy of inspiration, empowerment, and advancement that will influence the future even when the leaders are gone.

Chapter **20**

Grand Finale

Now that we have reached the pinnacle of our adventurous leadership journey, let me take a moment to express my sincere thanks for all of the amazing support and inspiration that I have received from you, my companions. Our trip was not a solo endeavour, but rather a group effort enhanced by the firm assistance of our loving family, the enduring faith of our faithful friends, and the wise guidance of our teachers. Their presence shone on our road, providing courage when we doubted ourselves and consolation when we felt uncertain. We have the deepest thanks for them.

Raising Little Leaders is a book comprising exciting stories with lessons, and activities, all of which have the purpose of developing leadership skills in children, beginning from the very basic understanding of the role of a leader and leadership qualities. As you turn the page, you will dive into the world of essential leadership concepts that you will learn in a child-friendly manner.

The first few chapters provide an overview of basic leadership concepts along with helpful stories and examples of youngsters who have shown leadership abilities. The following several chapters concentrate on developing future leaders through positive behaviour role-playing, leading by example, and assigning kids age-appropriate tasks within the context of the school.

Each concept is delivered with the sole purpose of encouraging children to add these qualities to them. From the significance of learning from mistakes to building self-esteem, relying on team members, actively listening, celebrating minor and major achievements and fostering a healthy and positive attitude towards self-development. Also, communication skills, irrespective of being verbal or non-verbal, are taught as they are a key quality in a leader. A young leader must be empathic, an effective communicator, an active listener, kind-hearted and many more.

Collaboration and teamwork have been highlighted as crucial elements of leadership, and experiences of how cooperation fosters creativity as well as solutions are given along with helpful advice on how to solve problems in a team environment. Other important topics included are emotional intelligence, kindness, goal-setting, time management, decision-making, conflict resolution, responsibility, and kindness; each has activities specifically designed for youngsters.

An interactive style is used throughout the book to keep young readers interested and to make learning fun. By the time the chapters are over, kids have a strong foundation in leadership, enabling them to grow into self-assured, kind, and capable leaders in a variety of contexts.

Let us develop a deep sense of gratitude for the numerous lessons we have learnt and the exceptional people who have aided in our development as we ponder. Every challenge we faced forged tenacity, flexibility, and an unshakable will to keep going in us. It was a furnace for our character. Let's pay tribute to the mentors who shared knowledge, the friends who provided support, and the life events that helped us become the leaders we are today.

Let's be a source of inspiration for each other as we prepare to embark on new journeys. Let's support people who walk the same route as us by freely sharing the wealth of wisdom and insights we have gained from our experience. We honour those who mentored us and continue the cycle of empowerment by stepping forward to be friends and mentors to future leaders. The future opens up in front of us like a bright painting, full of boundless options and possibilities. Let's seize the endless possibilities that lie ahead of us, driven by the unwavering belief that we can influence fate and bring about significant change.

I want to express my sincere appreciation to every one of my fellow travellers for adding to this journey with your unyielding devotion, fierce energy, and limitless excitement before we say goodbye. Our success as a group has been built on your presence, and for that, I am extremely grateful.

To sum up, I really hope that this journey has kindled a strong desire for leadership and constructive change in every one of us. May you always lead with honour, compassion, and unwavering bravery, shining your special light on the globe.

Let us, with steadfast resolution, carry forward the torch of leadership and forge a path of empowerment and enlightenment for future generations until we reunite on the waves of destiny. Goodbye, my dear friends, and may the winds of fate guide you to a future filled with success and happiness.